Building Character from the Start:

201 Activities

to foster creativity, literacy, and play in **K-3**

Susan Ragsdale and **Ann Saylor**

SEARCH
INSTITUTE
PRESS

Building Character from the Start: 201 Activities to Foster Creativity, Literacy, and Play in K–3.
Susan Ragsdale and Ann Saylor

The following are registered trademarks of Search Institute: Search Institute®, Developmental Assets®, and **HEALTHY YOUTH**®.

Search Institute Press, Minneapolis, MN
Copyright © 2009 by Susan Ragsdale and Ann Saylor

The content of this book has been reviewed by a number of K–3 professionals. Every effort has been made to provide sound direction for each game described herein. The authors, publisher, and reviewers take no responsibility for the use or misuse of any materials or methods described in this book, and will not be held liable for any injuries caused by participating in activities and games from this book. Please use prudent judgment and take appropriate safety precautions when participating in all activities and games.

10 9 8 7 6 5 4 3 2 1

Printed on acid-free paper in the United States of America.

Search Institute
615 First Avenue Northeast, Suite 125
Minneapolis, MN 55413
www.search-institute.org
612-376-8955 800-888-7828

ISBN-13: 978-1-57482-269-4

Credits
Editor: Alison Dotson
Book Design: Jeenee Lee
Production Supervisor: Mary Ellen Buscher

Library of Congress Cataloging-in-Publication Data

Ragsdale, Susan.
Building character from the start :
201 activities to foster creativity, literacy, and play in K-3 / Susan Ragsdale and Ann Saylor.
    p. cm.
ISBN-13: 978-1-57482-269-4 (pbk. : alk. paper)
ISBN-10: 1-57482-269-1 (pbk. : alk. paper)
1. Moral education (Primary)—United States.
2. Education, Primary—Activity programs—United States. I. Saylor, Ann. II. Title.
LC311.R34 2009
372.01'14—dc22
                                    2009015868

About Search Institute Press
Search Institute Press is a division of Search Institute, a nonprofit organization that offers leadership, knowledge, and resources to promote positive youth development. Our mission at Search Institute Press is to provide practical and hope-filled resources to help create a world in which all young people thrive. Our products are embedded in research, and the 40 Developmental Assets—qualities, experiences, and relationships youth need to succeed—are a central focus of our resources. Our logo, the SIP flower, is a symbol of the thriving and healthy growth young people experience when they have an abundance of assets in their lives.

CONTENTS

8 *Dedication*
9 *Acknowledgments*
11 *Introduction*
14 *The Framework of Developmental Assets*

17 UNIT ONE: FINISH THE PICTURES AND MASTERPIECE CREATIONS

Me and My Family
19 My Best Day
20 That's Funny!
21 My School
22 Let's Party!
23 Following the Rules
24 Fun at Home
25 Daily Chores

The People around Me
26 Caring Adults
27 Neighbors
28 You Are Special
29 Listening to Your Neighbors
30 Good Grown-Ups
31 Turn That Frown Upside Down!
32 School Trip
33 Healthy Choices
34 Let's Be Friends

My School
35 Schoolyard Friends
36 School Rules
37 Homework Help
38 Learning Is Fun!
39 Teacher for a Day
40 School Grown-Ups

All about Me
41 Good vs. Bad
42 Success!
43 Treasures in the Forest
44 After-School Activities
45 Religious Community
46 My Favorite Story
47 Standing Up
48 To Tell the Truth
49 Restaurant Opening
50 Look Both Ways
51 Making Up
52 Let Me Do It!
53 When I Grow Up

How I See Things
54 Being Neighborly
55 Home Safety
56 Around the World
57 Fashion Sense
58 Fairy Godmother

Favorite Books for Grades K-1

60   *All the Places to Love*
60   *A Bad Case of Stripes*
61   *A Box Can Be Many Things*
61   *Brown Bear, Brown Bear, What Do You See?*
62   *Chrysanthemum*
62   *Click Clack Moo: Cows That Type*
63   *The Cow That Went Oink*
63   *Dancing with Daddy*
64   *Dog Breath: The Horrible Trouble with Hally Tosis*
64   *Dora's Eggs*
65   *The Dot*
66   *Duck on a Bike*
66   *Elmer*
67   *Farm Flu*
67   *A Fish Out of Water*
68   *The Friend*
68   *The Gingerbread Man*
69   *Green Eggs and Ham*
69   *If You Give a Mouse a Cookie*
70   *I'm Gonna Like Me: Letting Off a Little Self-Esteem*
71   *Ish*
71   *Kiss the Cow!*
72   *Little by Little*
73   *Long Night Moon*

73   *Miss Nelson Is Missing!*
74   *Moe the Dog in Tropical Paradise*
74   *Mole Music*
75   *Not a Stick*
75   *The Other Side*
76   *Put Me in the Zoo*
76   *A Quiet Place*
77   *Something Might Happen*
77   *Stellaluna*
78   *Sunflower House*
79   *Those Can-Do Pigs*
79   *Today I Feel Silly and Other Moods That Make My Day*
80   *Tom's Tail*
80   *Tuesday*
81   *The Turn-Around, Upside-Down Alphabet Book*
82   *Walking through the Jungle*
82   *Wemberly Worried*
83   *When Sophie Gets Angry— Really, Really Angry*
83   *Wilfrid Gordon McDonald Partridge*
84   *Willy the Dreamer*

Favorite Books for Grades 2-3

85 *Alexander and the Terrible, Horrible, No Good, Very Bad Day*

85 *Appelemando's Dreams*

86 *Babushka, Baba Yaga*

87 *Book! Book! Book!*

87 *A Chair for My Mother*

88 *Clorinda*

88 *Cloudy with a Chance of Meatballs*

89 *Danny and the Dinosaur*

90 *Flat Stanley*

91 *Freckle Juice*

91 *The Great Fuzz Frenzy*

92 *The Hallo-Wiener*

92 *How to Make an Apple Pie and See the World*

93 *The Keeping Quilt*

93 *Koala Lou*

94 *Letting Swift River Go*

94 *The Magic Finger*

95 *Meet Danitra Brown*

95 *The Memory Coat*

96 *Mirette on the High Wire*

96 *The Mitten*

97 *The Mouse and the Motorcycle*

97 *Mr. Popper's Penguins*

98 *Mrs. Piggle-Wiggle*

98 *My Great-Aunt Arizona*

99 *My Rotten Redheaded Older Brother*

99 *The Paper Bag Princess*

100 *Pigsty*

100 *Pippi Longstocking*

101 *The Raft*

101 *Rechenka's Eggs*

102 *The Relatives Came*

102 *Roxaboxen*

103 *Sadako and the Thousand Paper Cranes*

103 *Saturdays and Teacakes*

104 *The Spyglass: A Book about Faith*

104 *Stella Louella's Runaway Book*

105 *The Stories Julian Tells*

105 *Thunder Cake*

106 *Toys Go Out: Being the Adventures of a Knowledgeable Stingray, a Toughy Little Buffalo, and Someone Called Plastic*

106 *Train to Somewhere*

107 *The True Story of the Three Little Pigs*

108 *The Velveteen Rabbit*

108 *Weslandia*

109 *When Jessie Came across the Sea*

109 *The Wonderful Happens*

110 *Yoko*

Community-Building Games

113 Human Bingo
113 Hot Potato Toss
114 I Know You, Friend!
114 Smile
115 I Like People Who Like . . .
115 My Friend
116 Spinning a Yarn
116 Cub Reporter
117 What Makes Me "Me"
117 Gossip or Telephone

Word Games

118 Give Me an A! B! C!
118 Spelling Beat
118 ABC Stack-Up
119 What's in a Word?
120 Rhymes Scramble
120 The Changing Word Game
121 Alphabet Soup
121 Collaborative Writers
    121 Round One: Word Wizards
    122 Round Two: Sentence Starters
    122 Round Three: Story Stacks
122 By the Roll
123 Story Perspectives
124 Portable Words
124 Impromptu Authors
125 Build a Body

Follow the Leader Games

126 Red Light, Green Light
126 Bubble Gum Light
127 Teacher Says
127 Follow the Leader
127 Contrary Leaders
127 The Review Line Game
128 Space Travel

Artsy Games

128 Collaborative Song Writers
129 Superheroes Live and in Action!
129 Human Band
130 Back Drawings
130 An Artist's Tale
131 Hidden Treasures
131 Alphabet Pictures
132 Animal Charades

Energizing Games

133 Workout Rolls
133 Cinderella's Shoes

Puzzle Games

134 Clang Clang
134 Guessing Game
135 I Spy

Team-Building Games

136 Superhero Team Relay
138 Stack-Up Cups
138 Tug of War
138 Group Roll
139 Balloon Keep-Up
139 Beep Beep!
140 Station Relay

Backward Play

140 Animal Match
141 Backward Dress
141 Backward Lineup
142 Over/Under Pass

Olympics

142 Disc Throw
142 Javelin Throw
143 Frisbee Throw
143 Long Jump
143 Long Jump Relay
143 Jumping Frog Variation

Marathon Events

144 Jumping Jacks
144 Running in Place
144 Sit-Ups
144 Push-Ups
144 Squats
144 Nonstop Talking
144 Joke Telling
144 Stare-Downs
145 Bet You Can't Be Quiet!

Scavenger Hunts

145 Holiday Scavenger Hunt
146 News Scavenger Hunt
146 These-Two-Things Scavenger Hunt

149 *Asset Index*

DEDICATION

To kids everywhere, may you develop a lifelong passion and love
for play, creativity, fantasy, and exploring imaginary worlds.

To Pete, the "big kid" in my life, thanks for filling my life with laughter,
play, and ongoing antics that keep me on my toes. —*Susan*

To my three children—Daniel (7), Brendan (4), and Anna Kate (2)—
who continually inspire the creative spirit within me.

To my loving husband, who lets me be my crazy, creative self
and pursue my sometimes crazy dreams! —*Ann*

ACKNOWLEDGMENTS

To our art and play team who embraced this project with joy, energy, and enthusiasm, shared their favorite games, dreamed up possibilities, and gave from sage wisdom and experience for crafting just the right questions to engage children and adults together in joyful conversation. Sujette Overstreet, Sandy Gilbert, Rob Sasser, Russ Harris, Paris Goodyear-Brown, and Lynn Hutcheson—you are all wonderful and special gifts to the children lucky enough to be in your lives! And to Sam Goodyear-Brown, age 7, it was a treat to have your thoughtful input on the art section.

To the book connoisseurs who shared their favorite books and their enthusiasm for why these books are the best ever! With you, we were able to conspire and craft new ways to make books come alive and spent hours in animated conversations of pure fun. You helped to make this collection great. We give a special thanks to Lana Settle—you have hugely blessed this work!

To our young commentators and avid readers: Daniel and Brendan Saylor, ages 7 and 4; Miranda and Marcella Jones, ages 12 and 9; Nicholas and Sara Ann McClain, ages 9 and 7; Chad Thomas, age 8; Sarah and Andrew Hunter, ages 13 and 10; and Ella Johnstad, age 8, thank you for taking the time to share your special books with us. Kids around the world will be grateful for your input!

And thanks to our big kid book connoisseur contributors: Linda Tupper, Marci McClain, Amy Anderson, Dana McIntosh, Kristin Johnstad and Bill Richmond, Pam Hunter, Peggy Saylor, Shannon Truss, Susan Poulter, Windee Robinson, and Melanie Jones.

Final thanks and heartfelt appreciation go out to the usual suspects who help make our work a reality: Bucky Rosenbaum, Alison Dotson, Tenessa Gemelke, Mary Ellen Buscher, and Bill Kauffmann.

INTRODUCTION

Creativity is our entryway to other worlds. It can take us to amazing places where we can fly atop dragons, converse with talking frogs, meet and befriend new races (of plants, dinosaurs, giants, mice, unicorns, wizards, and so many more), or even picnic with the King of Ants in a celebratory truce of battles.

Once we open the doors to imagination, our minds become like portals. We never know where we'll find ourselves—in the middle of a battlefield with spoon in hand trying to save a gang of flying squirrels? Flying through the house, cape flapping behind as we seek to banish the monster that comes out at night and disturbs our sleep? Or sitting at the feet of a wise, tattered rabbit, listening intently as she recounts how one becomes real to a bunch of eager toys? The possibilities are endless.

Color, art, imagery—each has its special way of taking us to the kaleidoscopic inner world of creativity where we can roam, explore, discover, and be transformed by what we encounter. With art, we are invited to share with the world what we see with the eyes of the artist inside us. One person's folded-up piece of paper is another person's hair bow, another one's mustache, and yet another's butterfly. A simple cloud or moon in the eyes of an adult may for a cloud-gazing child be an elephant tromping through a field of grass, or for a stargazer, a wolf chasing the boy in the moon.

It's all in the eyes and the world of the beholder.

With the art of books, we encounter authors who transport us into worlds of the mind and imagination. They gather us in and involve us in the story from the onset. Is there a battle between good and evil? Is someone in trouble and only we can help? When books come alive, we enter into their stories to explore our own values, cheer on our heroes, defeat the villains, discover hidden meanings for ourselves, and learn the world's lessons and truths. When we enter into stories, we become part of the stories, and truth be told, they may very well become part of us.

Then, when we leave their worlds (and alas, we must return to our own!), we bring with us something more, something satisfying and fulfilling that is always ours to treasure and hold. Perhaps it's a nugget of truth or self-discovery, or maybe it's a sense of value or a lesson in character that sticks with us. Or maybe, just maybe, it's a lifelong friendship with reading that we keep forever.

In that outer world, we find that creativity and self-discovery can and do occur in the hands and at the direction of children in the midst of play. We cannot always have our noses in books or hands in paint! We must sometimes come up for air—get up, move, interact, socialize, energize, de-stress, make friends, laugh, and share. And what better way than through play—to actively engage with others and learn life's lessons through games?

Play is at the very heart of how children learn and interact with the world around them. Playing make-believe, for example, that "free-for-all" kind of play in which children create their own scenarios, weave their own stories, and determine their own dialogue and outcomes, is an opportunity for children to improvise and develop skills, both cognitive and social, that expand their capacity for thinking and learning as well as for creativity and imagination.

Within the pages of this book are art pieces to finish, books to read, and activities to do that let children explore more fully the fantastic dimensions of creativity, stories, and play. These activities can be used to help children tap the fertile imagination within, cultivate inner creativity and self-expression, discover and build character, and, hopefully, find a lifelong love for creating, drawing, reading, writing, and playing. Children can finish the picture as they see fit, bring books to life through conversations and activities that add depth to the written word, and play games that stimulate their minds, engage their restless bodies, and inspire their unhindered spirits. The units of this book follow that format: finish pictures, bring books to life, and play. Unit One focuses on art and creating "masterpieces." Along with these masterpieces are age-appropriate questions to engage children in conversations about their artwork and their lives. Unit Two seeks to build literacy skills through reading and writing. It too provides a venue for children and adults to converse, dream, and play together. Unit Three ensures that we meet the need children have to move and express themselves through physical activity by focusing on the power of play. Again, the games found here include age-appropriate conversation starters to help children explore what they are learning and discovering during their time at play.

The tools of imagination that this book highlights—creativity, literacy, and play—are important for helping us identify the strengths and interests of the children around us. As you go through the activities in this book, watch and learn. What makes children respond and come alive? Does art or story or play bring out a spirit of enthusiasm? Do any of these things energize a particular child or group of children? Watch for the stories, games, or art pieces that children want to return to again and again. Note their preferences. Note how they act and what they say about themselves in response to what is going on. Then build on the strengths and interests you've identified to provide further opportunities for stimulation and growth.

The pages of this book were crafted with one ear tuned in to the world of imagination and one eye turned toward what research tells us is vital for children to be vibrant, strong, and true. Used intentionally, the tools of imagination can help mold and shape the character and inner strengths of young children. Character-building moments are woven throughout every page in this book in both subtle and direct ways. As children finish the pictures, they must find within themselves the things they value and put to paper how they see the world. The picture becomes complete as you chat with children about their creation and ask questions to help them think through their take on the world. The act of creating itself builds character as children practice something they love (or for some, gain a new skill and practice getting better at something they may not excel at) and gain confidence in self-expression. In addition, children have multiple opportunities to clarify and talk about values and character through the various stories, activities, and games they experience. Questions and opportunities to share are included after each as a guide, so you can help children make the connection between what they just participated in and life itself. Those conversations will be chock-full of character-building moments because the questions were intentionally crafted with the 40 Developmental Assets in mind. And wherever you find assets, you will find character.

At the end of this book on page 149 is a list of Search Institute's 40 Developmental Assets for children, a research-based list of factors needed in all children's lives to help them thrive, a must-have for helping children become who they're meant to be. Put to use, the asset framework can become a part of what you do with children every day, too. (For more ideas on how you can include the assets in your work with children, go to search-institute.org and theassetedge.net.) The Developmental Assets framework connects those fantastic inner-fantasy worlds explored inside this book with healthy doses of positive youth development.

Every activity denotes the asset(s) to which it relates, thus connecting creative sparks with developmental sparks. As you go through these pages, all the dots will be connected. You will see how art, books, and play lend themselves to building assets and character (for values *are* a part of the assets children need, and when children have caring adults and opportunities to express themselves and explore, character-clarifying moments naturally tend to happen) as well as creativity and self-expression within children. In short, this book is all about teachable moments. You can use each moment of each activity to pass on lessons that will last a lifetime: lessons of love, lessons of life, and lessons of character—right from the start.

THE FRAMEWORK OF DEVELOPMENTAL ASSETS FOR CHILDREN GRADES K-3 (AGES 5-9)

EXTERNAL ASSETS

Support

1. *Family Support*—Family continues to be a consistent provider of love and support for the child's unique physical and emotional needs.

2. *Positive Family Communication*—Parent(s) and child communicate openly, respectfully, and frequently, with child receiving praise for her or his efforts and accomplishments.

3. *Other Adult Relationships*—Child receives support from adults other than her or his parent(s), with the child sometimes experiencing relationships with a nonparent adult.

4. *Caring Neighborhood*—Parent(s) and child experience friendly neighbors who affirm and support the child's growth and sense of belonging.

5. *Caring School Climate*—Child experiences warm, welcoming relationships with teachers, caregivers, and peers at school.

6. *Parent Involvement in Schooling*—Parent(s) talk about the importance of education and are actively involved in the child's school success.

Empowerment

7. *Community Values Children*—Children are welcomed and included throughout community life.

8. *Children as Resources*—Child contributes to family decisions and has opportunities to participate in positive community events.

9. *Service to Others*—Child has opportunities to serve in the community with adult support and approval.

10. *Safety*—Parents and community adults ensure the child's safety while keeping in mind her or his increasing independence.

Boundaries and Expectations

11. *Family Boundaries*—The family maintains supervision of the child, has reasonable guidelines for behavior, and always knows where the child is.

12. *School Boundaries*—Schools have clear, consistent rules and consequences and use a positive approach to discipline.

13. *Neighborhood Boundaries*—Neighbors and friends' parents help monitor the child's behavior and provide feedback to the parent(s).

14. *Adult Role Models*—Parent(s) and other adults model positive, responsible behavior and encourage the child to follow these examples.

15. *Positive Peer Influence*—Parent(s) monitor the child's friends and encourage spending time with those who set good examples.

16. *High Expectations*—Parent(s), teachers, and other influential adults encourage the child to do her or his best in all tasks and celebrate their successes.

Constructive Use of Time

17. *Creative Activities*—Child participates weekly in music, dance, or other form of artistic expression outside of school.

18. *Child Programs*—Child participates weekly in at least one sport, club, or organization within the school or community.

19. *Religious Community*—Child participates in age-appropriate religious activities and caring relationships that nurture her or his spiritual development.

20. *Time at Home*—Child spends time at home playing and doing positive activities with the family.

Commitment to Learning

21. *Achievement Motivation*—Child is encouraged to remain curious and demonstrates an interest in doing well at school.

22. *Learning Engagement*—Child is enthused about learning and enjoys going to school.

23. *Homework*—With appropriate parental support, child completes assigned homework.

24. *Bonding to School*—Child is encouraged to have and feels a sense of belonging at school.

25. *Reading for Pleasure*—Child listens to and/or reads books outside of school daily.

Positive Values

26. *Caring*—Parent(s) help child grow in empathy, understanding, and helping others.

27. *Equality and Social Justice*—Parent(s) encourage child to be concerned about rules and being fair to everyone.

28. *Integrity*—Parent(s) help child develop her or his own sense of right and wrong behavior.

29. *Honesty*—Parent(s) encourage child's development in recognizing and telling the truth.

30. *Responsibility*—Parent(s) encourage child to accept and take responsibility for her or his actions at school and at home.

31. *Self-Regulation*—Parents encourage child's growth in regulating her or his own emotions and behaviors and in understanding the importance of healthy habits and choices.

Social Competencies

32. *Planning and Decision Making*—Parent(s) help child think through and plan school and play activities.

33. *Interpersonal Competence*—Child seeks to build friendships and is learning about self-control.

34. *Cultural Competence*—Child continues to learn about her or his own cultural identity and is encouraged to interact positively with children of different racial, ethnic, and cultural backgrounds.

35. *Resistance Skills*—Child is learning to recognize risky or dangerous situations and is able to seek help from trusted adults.

36. *Peaceful Conflict Resolution*—Child continues learning to resolve conflicts without hitting, throwing a tantrum, or using hurtful language.

Positive Identity

37. *Personal Power*—Child has a growing sense of having influence over some of the things that happen in her or his life.

38. *Self-Esteem*—Child likes herself or himself and feels valued by others.

39. *Sense of Purpose*—Child welcomes new experiences and imagines what he or she might do or be in the future.

40. *Positive View of Personal Future*—Child has a growing curiosity about the world and finding her or his place in it.

Finish the Picture and Masterpiece Creations

Art is a medium that lets everyone play. And because beauty lies in the eye of the beholder, art is also an equalizer that allows anyone to craft and create.

Through creative activities, children have the opportunity to explore their artistic side, and through adult and peer encouragement and support in completing such activities, children reap the rewards of self-discovery and the belief in their own abilities. In the following pages, you will find a variety of pictures waiting to be finished. These picture "starts" are meant to encourage budding illustrators and artists, both timid and bold, in their efforts toward artistic expression. They can be completed as each young artist sees fit.

The picture activities are arranged in five categories, each allowing children to express an aspect of how they view themselves as well as the people and world around them. You'll find pictures and activities for your children under Me and My Family, The People around Me, My School, All about Me, and How I See Things.

At the beginning of each picture activity is the asset to which it is matched—those that connect the experience of creativity with well-being and positive development. Each picture includes one or more questions, under the heading of Let's Talk, to use as follow-up after the activity. These questions will help you see what your budding artists see and will help give both meaning and value to what seems to the children like just a fun picture to draw. In some instances, the picture activities are followed with a book icon and a suggested companion book to naturally connect the idea of the picture with a story included in Unit Two.

When well tended, the inner traits of imagination, creativity, and discovery contribute to a child's overall character and well-being. Creative activities can help children thrive in their everyday lives.

My Best Day

Draw a picture of the best day you have had with your family.

FAMILY SUPPORT
FOCUS ON ASSETS
1

What did you do that was fun?
Who or what made this the best day?

This picture page connects well to the book *Dancing with Daddy* by Willy Welch. See page 63.

That's Funny!

Draw a picture of something that makes your family laugh.

Let's Talk

What is happening in your picture? Did this really happen?
What other things make you and your family laugh together?

My School

Draw a picture of yourself and your parent(s) at your school.

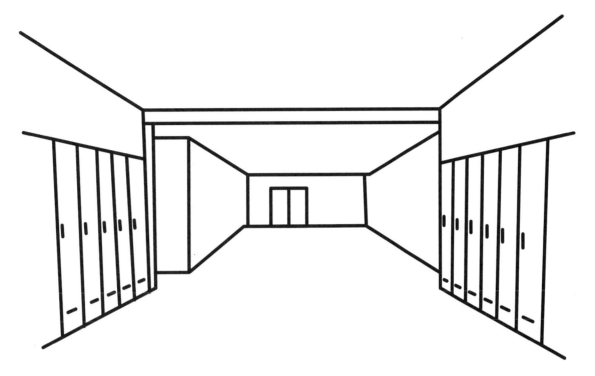

Let's Talk

Where is your favorite place to be at school? Why do you like this spot? What one thing or person do you want your parents to see? Why?

Let's Party!

Draw a picture of your family at a party.

Let's Talk

Why are you having the party? Who will you ask to come?
What food will you have? What games will you play?

Following the Rules

Draw a picture of yourself in a room of your home.

flush the toilet

don't jump on the couch

Let's Talk

Does your family have a rule for this room? What is the rule? Why do you think it's important? What are some other rules you have at home?

Fun at Home

Draw a picture of something you really like to do at home.

 **Let's Talk**

Why is this thing you do special to you? Which family members do this with you? How often do you do this?

This drawing activity connects well to the book *Saturdays and Teacakes* by Lester L. Laminack. See page 103.

Daily Chores

Draw a chore you have to do at home.

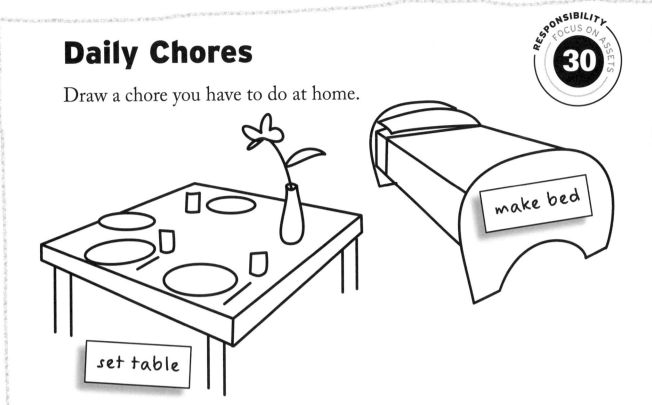

set table

make bed

Let's Talk

Do you have a job or chore that people count on you to do?
What is this job? Why is it *your* job? Who asked you to do it?
How does it help others?

Caring Adults

Draw the people who
take care of you when
your family is not around.

(**Let's Talk**)

Who are these people? How do
they help you? What do you like
about them? How do they make
you feel?

This drawing activity connects
well with the book *The Friend* by
Sarah Stewart. See page 68.

Neighbors

Draw a picture of your neighbors.

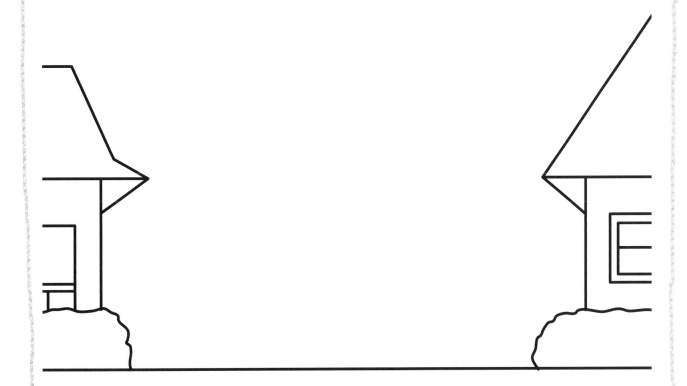

What do your neighbors do for you that you like?

Which neighbor do you like to see and talk with the most?

What makes this neighbor your favorite?

You Are Special

These kids are getting an award for doing something very special. Draw a picture or write in what the award is for.

Let's Talk

Who are these children? What did they do?
Who is giving them the award?

Listening to Your Neighbors

Draw a picture or write in what your neighbor would say if you were doing something you're not supposed to do.

Let's Talk

Why would your neighbor say this to you?

Which neighbors care about what happens to you?

Which neighbors are your family's friends?

Good Grown-Ups

Do you know a grown-up you really like?
Draw a picture of this grown-up and write the things
you like about this person.

"Grown-Up"   "Me"

Let's Talk

Who is this grown-up? Why do you want to be like this person?
What does this grown-up do that is so good or special?

Turn That Frown Upside Down!

This little boy looks sad. Draw a picture or write about what you would do to cheer him up.

What did you do to try to make him feel better? Did it work? Why or why not? How do you feel when you help others? How do other people try to cheer you up?

School Trip

Pretend you are taking a school trip. There are not enough lunches for everyone, but you get one. Draw a picture or write about what you will do to help the kids without lunch.

Let's Talk

What did you do to help? Did everyone get food to eat? Did everyone share? Talk about a time you shared something of yours with someone else.

Healthy Choices

This picture shows kids making healthy choices.
Color two of the choices you would make.

Let's Talk

Why are these kids' actions healthy choices? What is something you do to be healthy? Why do people exercise? What are other things besides exercise that people can do to be healthy?

Let's Be Friends

This picture shows someone sitting alone. Draw a picture or write about what you would do to make friends with the person.

What did you do to make friends with this person? What did the two of you talk about? How did it feel to make a new friend?

Schoolyard Friends

Draw a picture of some kids who go to your school.

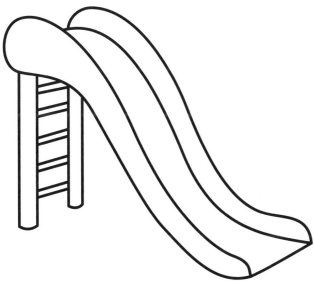

What do these kids like to do? Do you play with them?
Do you eat lunch with them? What do you like about each one?

School Rules

Write down or draw some of the other school rules that you follow.

Keep hands to yourself.

-
-
-

Walk, don't run.

-
-
-

Share with others.

-
-
-

(Let's Talk)

Why are the rules you wrote down easy to follow? What other rules does your school have? Which rules do you and your friends have a hard time following? Why?

This picture page connects well to the book *Miss Nelson Is Missing!* by Harry Allard. See page 73.

Homework Help

This teacher is helping a girl with schoolwork that she doesn't understand. Color this picture.

Let's Talk

Do you ask for help when you don't understand something in school? How does your teacher help you?

Learning Is Fun!

Draw a picture of something that makes learning at school fun.

A B C D E F G H I J K L M N O P Q R S T U V W X Y Z

a b c d e f g h i j k l m n o p q r s t u v w x y z

 **Let's Talk**

What makes learning fun for you? What does the teacher do to make it fun? What do other kids have fun doing at school? Do you like doing these things?

Teacher for a Day

Pretend you are the teacher for a day.
Write what homework you will give the class.

Today's homework assignment

 **Let's Talk**

What homework did you give the class? Why did you pick this as homework? Do you think the students understood what they are supposed to do? What can you do to make sure all the students do their homework?

School Grown-Ups

Draw a picture of your favorite grown-up at school.

principal

janitor

lunch worker

My favorite person at school

Let's Talk

Who did you draw? Why did you pick this person as your favorite? Does this person get you excited to go to school? Why?

Good vs. Bad

Think of a time when you and a friend saw something or were in a situation that meant choosing between doing something good and doing something bad. Draw a picture of the situation and the choice you made.

Who was with you? What did you see or what happened that left you with a choice to make? What did you decide to do? What else could you have done? Why was what you did the right or wrong thing?

Success!

Think of something you didn't believe you could do that somebody told you you could do and you *did*. Draw a picture of what you did.

Why didn't you think you could do this? Who encouraged you to try? What is something else you're not sure you could do, but would like to try next? Who can help you?

This drawing activity works well with the book *Clorinda* by Robert Kinerk. See page 88.

HIGH EXPECTATIONS
FOCUS ON ASSETS
16

Treasures in the Forest

The forest in this picture has many special things or treasures to collect. Draw a picture of what you would like to collect if you went for a walk through this forest.

Let's Talk

Why would you like to collect this? What is something neat or special about this collection? What other things would you like to collect?

This works well with the book *The Mitten* by Jan Brett. See page 96.

After-School Activities

Draw a picture of a fun activity you like to do after school.

What do you like about the activity you drew? What other things do you do for fun after school? Why do you like these activities?

Religious Community

Some families visit a mosque, church, synagogue, or temple where they get to know lots of people. Draw a picture of this place or another place your family goes to spend time with people.

Let's Talk

What happens at this place? What do you like about this place?

My Favorite Story

Draw a picture from a story you really like
to have read to you.

Let's Talk

What is the title of the story? What is the story about?
What other stories do you like? What do you like about them?
Does someone read to you each day? Do you read to anyone?

Standing Up

This picture shows someone helping a friend who was getting picked on by others. Color it.

Have you ever helped a friend who was getting picked on? What happened? How do you think your friend felt when you helped? How did it feel to help your friend? Has anyone ever helped you like this? What happened?

This coloring activity connects well to *The Cow That Went Oink* by Bernard Most. See page 63.

To Tell the Truth

Draw a picture about a time when someone told a lie.

Let's Talk

Talk about a time you told the truth when it was hard to do. How did you feel after telling the truth? Who helps you tell the truth? Why do you think telling the truth is important?

This drawing activity connects well to the book *The True Story of the Three Little Pigs* by Jon Scieszka. See page 107.

Restaurant Opening

Pretend you are starting a new restaurant. Draw a picture of the food you will serve.

Let's Talk

What is the name of your restaurant? What are you serving? Why did you pick this food? Do you think a lot of people will like this food?

This drawing activity connects well to the book *Yoko* by Rosemary Wells. See page 110.

Look Both Ways

The girl in this picture is keeping herself safe. Draw a picture of something dangerous in the street.

Let's Talk

Name some things you do to keep yourself safe.

What are things you've been taught to do to stay safe?

Have you ever wanted to do something unsafe but stopped yourself from doing it? How did you do that?

Making Up

Pretend you are mad at a friend. Draw a picture that shows you and your friend after you have made up and are friends again.

 **Let's Talk**

What did your friend do to make you mad? What did you do to become friends again? What will you do next time if you and your friend start to get mad at each other?

This drawing activity connects well to *The Magic Finger* by Roald Dahl (see page 94) and *My Rotten Redheaded Older Brother* by Patricia Polacco (see page 99).

Let Me Do It!

 Draw a picture of something you can do all by yourself.

 **Let's Talk**

What can you do all by yourself?
How did you learn to do it?
How does it feel to be able to
do it by yourself?

 This drawing activity connects
well to the book *Those Can-Do
Pigs* by David McPhail. See
page 79.

When I Grow Up

Pretend you are grown up. Draw or write about something special you hope to do.

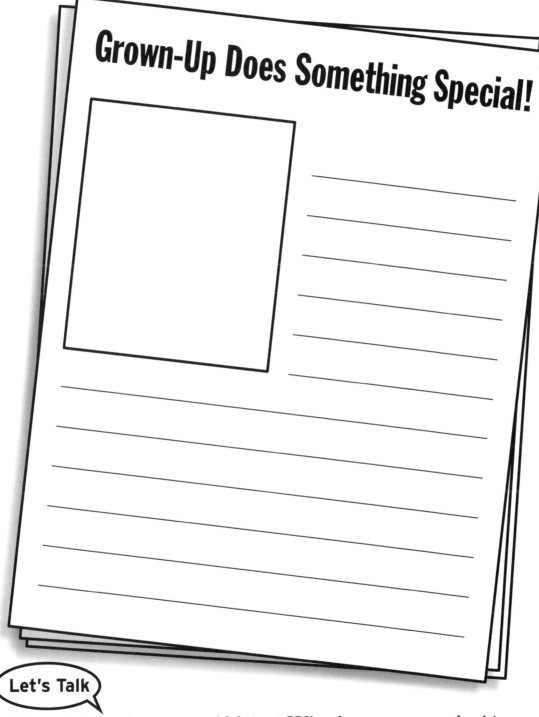

Grown-Up Does Something Special!

Let's Talk

What did you draw yourself doing? Why do you want to do this special thing when you are grown up?

Being Neighborly

Imagine that your neighbor is sick or hurt. Draw a picture of your neighbor and what you would do to help her.

 **Let's Talk**

Which neighbor did you draw? What made you want to help this person? What are you doing to help? How does it make your neighbor feel?

This drawing activity works well with the book *Wilfrid Gordon McDonald Partridge* by Mem Fox. See page 83.

Home Safety

Draw a picture of what makes your home safe.

Let's Talk

What do you and your family members do to make your home safe?
How do these things make it safe?

Around the World

Draw a place you would like to visit and learn more about.

What do you know about this place? Why do you want to go there? What will you do when you get there?

Fashion Sense

Pretend you are visiting another planet, and you have to wear clothes that show people who you are and what you like. Draw a picture of the clothes you would wear.

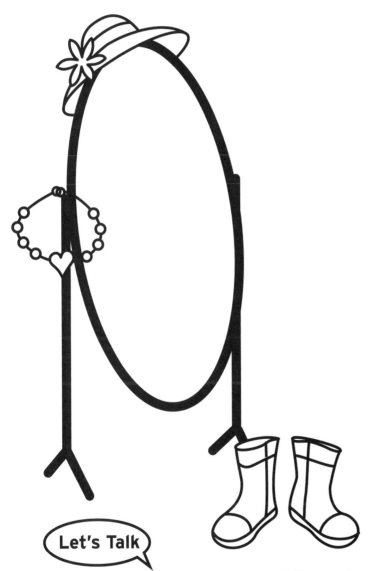

Let's Talk

What clothes did you pick? What colors did you choose?
Why did you pick these clothes and these colors?
What will people think about you when they see you in these clothes?
What makes your clothes special?

Fairy Godmother

Your fairy godmother gives you three wishes for the world. Draw a picture or write about your three wishes.

Let's Talk

What are your three wishes? Why are these wishes important to you?

Experiencing Books

Picture books have a magical way of opening up new worlds to children and adults alike. Reading one with a caring adult presents a natural opportunity for a child to talk about the book and apply its lessons to everyday life and learning. Many books also invite readers to explore their content through a variety of creative activities—journaling, painting, playing games, building, dreaming, and writing.

This section describes favorite picture books, divided into categories for readers in grades K–1 and readers in grades 2–3. After each title, you will find a brief description of the book; "Let's Talk," several questions for discussion and/or writing prompts; and "Explore More," a collection of activities and experiences that help bring the book to life.

Use the questions as a guideline to help children explore various components of the story. Let them fuel your conversation and lead to self-discovery, character exploration, and relationship building. The questions can also be used as writing prompts for journals, reports, or essays to further build literacy skills.

All the Places to Love

by Patricia MacLachlan
illustrated by Michael Wimmer

Eli lives with his grandparents on a big farm, where he forms bonds with all its special places—the valley, meadows, and river—and, of course, his family.

Let's Talk

- What are your family's traditions (things you do every night or during every holiday)?

- What special items are important to your family? Why are they special?

- What does it mean when we say we are "passing down" things in our family (like a ring or a piece of furniture)?

Explore More

- Ask children to think about their most treasured possessions. Then ask them to write a story about one of these possessions and how they will pass it down to their children and grandchildren.

- Discuss different kinds of holidays—religious, national, cultural—and have children make a list of the ways their family celebrates one of those holidays. Children can read their list to the class. Ask them if they've learned of any new holiday traditions their own family could adopt.

- Prompt the children to think of their family traditions. Have them draw a picture of their favorite family tradition to take home to hang on the refrigerator or in their bedroom. Ask them if there are any new traditions they would like their family to try, and encourage them to suggest the new ideas to their family.

Focus on Assets
1: Family Support

A Bad Case of Stripes

by David Shannon

Camilla worries so much about what other kids think of her that she breaks out in stripes all over her body. But stripes are just the beginning—she is also plagued with roots, berries, tree limbs, feathers, and a tail. In the end, the only solution is to be true to herself.

Let's Talk

- What is something special about you that makes you a little bit different from other people?

- What do you like that no one else likes?

- Why is it good to be different from other people sometimes?

- What would the world be like if we all looked alike and all liked the same things?

Explore More

- Have children make a nameplate using construction paper, glue, glitter, markers, and stickers. Tell them their nameplate should show their personality and be made to look unique. Let children keep their nameplate on their desk or cubby.

- Have the children write a short poem. Help them highlight ways that they are special. One way you can do this is to have them write a poem using an adjective that describes them for each letter of their first name.

Focus on Assets
34: Cultural Competence
38: Self-Esteem

A Box Can Be Many Things

by Dana Meachen Rau

Their mother may think the box she throws away is just a box, but her children know better—it easily transforms into a bear cave, a car, a house, and a cage. The more the box breaks down, the more creative the children get.

Let's Talk

- What was your favorite box creation in this book?

- If you could make your own toy out of anything, what would it be? What would you use to make the toy?

- Do you like to make your own toys to play with? Why or why not?

Explore More

- Give children an empty shoe box (or any box) and have them think of new ways to play with it. Provide paper, markers, crayons, and glue for children to decorate their box, and then have each child share her "not a box" story with the class.

- Play a creative thinking game. See "Hidden Treasures" in the games section on page 131.

Check out the companion book *Christina Katerina and the Box* by Patricia Lee Gauch.

Focus on Assets
1: Family Support
11: Family Boundaries
32: Planning and Decision Making

Brown Bear, Brown Bear, What Do You See?

by Bill Martin Jr.
illustrated by Eric Carle

Not only are the illustrations in this classic book captivating and memorable, but the rhymes will stick with children and get them excited about reading. With each turn of a page, children encounter a new animal that inspires them to continue.

Let's Talk

- What are some differences you see in the animals?

- Why do you think we are all different?

- What would it be like if everyone were the same?

Explore More

- Gather small pieces of colored scrap paper so children can create collages that reflect the patchwork-style characters in *Brown Bear, Brown Bear.* Encourage children to be creative, and give them permission to make animals that don't actually exist.

- Say: *What's your favorite color? What's your favorite animal? Create an imaginary animal that combines your favorite color and your favorite animal, then make up a silly story about it. Draw pictures of your story.*

- Have children make up stories with their own characters. For example, you could say, "Judy, Judy, what do you see? I see Ann looking at me." Then encourage the children to come up with their own.

- When you read this book again, try singing it out loud.

Focus on Assets
34: Cultural Competence

Chrysanthemum
by Kevin E. Henkes

Chrysanthemum has loving parents who help her feel special about herself and her name, which they say matches her perfectly. But when she enters kindergarten, the little mouse sees her name in a new perspective: it is strange and long and deserves to be made fun of by her classmates. It isn't until her beloved teacher announces to the class that she will name her baby after Chrysanthemum that the students realize the name has its merits—and so does the mouse who bears it.

Let's Talk

• How did the other mice make Chrysanthemum feel?

• How did her feelings change by the end of the story?

• Have you ever made fun of someone's name, or something else about that person? How do you think that made the person feel? How would *you* feel?

• How would you stand up for a friend if someone else was picking on him?

Explore More

• Provide felt or paper, paints, glue, glitter, markers, or beads for children to make a monogram of their name. If time or supplies are limited, have children design just their first initial.

• Have children create a crazy name and ask them to write a story about or draw a picture of their new character.

• Ask children to make up* a story about their name's origin, and put the stories up on bulletin boards. Have students use a microphone (a marker or paper towel tube) to conduct mock interviews with each other regarding their made-up stories.

* For some children, providing a true account of their name origin can be a sensitive topic.

Adopted children may not know the origin of their given names, and children living in foster care or with a relative may not have an opportunity to ask their parents for the story.

Focus on Assets

33: Interpersonal Competence
36: Peaceful Conflict Resolution
38: Self-Esteem

Click Clack Moo: Cows That Type
by Doreen Cronin
illustrated by Betsy Lewin

Hilarity ensues when farm cows find a typewriter and learn to use it to demand better treatment from Farmer Brown, who is shocked and irritated. When the farmer refuses the cows' request for electric blankets to keep warm at night, they go on strike, and the opposing sides employ a neutral duck to mediate.

Let's Talk

• What was the silliest part of this book?

• Which animal did you like the best? Why?

• Why is it important for us to learn to read and write?

Explore More

• Whisper a random animal name into each child's ear. For example, whisper *pig* to one child and *cow* to the next. Ask children to

THE EXPERTS WEIGH IN

"This story makes my girls laugh out loud every time!"

Amy Anderson, teacher, owner of Let's Explore, and mother of two form animal groups without talking. They can "oink" and "moo" as sounds— but they can't use words.

- Role-play with the children. Give each student a part to play from *Click Clack Moo* as it is read. Every time a character is mentioned, the children should make a corresponding sound and motion. If someone is the farmer, he might say, "Yee haw." If someone is the duck, she can waddle and quack.

- Talk about products people tend to buy at the grocery store and trace them back to their origin. Ask: *Where does milk come from? Where do eggs come from? What about potatoes? Bread? Honey? Peanut butter? What about chocolate milk?*

- Play Animal Match. Find instructions on page 140.

Focus on Assets
27: Equality and Social Justice
32: Planning and Decision Making
37: Personal Power

The Cow That Went Oink
by Bernard Most

A cow who can say only "oink," not "moo," must endure being made fun of and laughed at by the other cows—that is, until she meets a pig who can moo but cannot oink. They teach each other how to say "moo" and "oink" and end up with twice the vocabulary of the animals who once laughed at them.

Let's Talk

- Has anyone ever laughed at you for being different? How did it make you feel?

- Have you ever laughed at anyone else for being different? How do you think it made that person feel?

Explore More

- Instruct children to sculpt their favorite farm animals out of clay or dough. Display the animals (the school library is a good place), then open up the "art gallery" for other students and school staff to visit. You can take this activity even further by inviting parents to view the art, during either a school day or a parent-teacher conference.

- Play Animal Match on page 140 or What Makes Me "Me" on page 117.

Focus on Assets
26: Caring
27: Equality and Social Justice
33: Interpersonal Competence
38: Self-Esteem

Dancing with Daddy
by Willy Welch
illustrated by Liza Woodruff

Daddy and daughter joyfully dance out of the house and all the way into the forest, where animals, trees, and fireflies join in and sway along with them.

Let's Talk

- Why did the little girl think the trees and animals were dancing?

- What makes you feel like dancing?

- What other things do you think trees and animals like to do with people?

- What's your favorite thing to do with your mom or dad, or the person who lives with you and takes care of you?

Explore More

- Make up your own dance steps with a partner, then teach the dance to the children. Say: *Pretend you started dancing without trying to. Imagine all the places your dancing feet took you.*

- Give each child a piece of paper. Say: *Fold the paper in half. Now fold it in half again. There should now be four sections. In each of the sections, draw one of the best places you visited while dancing like crazy.*

- Find a quiet place to sit outside. Have children make a list of all the things they see "dancing" (or running or singing or waving).

- Have children create a story about what trees and animals like to do together when people are not watching.

Focus on Assets
1: Family Support
3: Other Adult Relationships
17: Creative Activities

Dog Breath: The Horrible Trouble with Hally Tosis
by Dav Pilkey

Hally Tosis is a dog with breath so foul that Grandma falls off her chair upon catching a whiff of it. When Hally's human parents decide to give him up for adoption, the children of the family embark on several crazy adventures in an attempt to keep their beloved pet. In the end, Hally saves his family from burglars and wins their acceptance.

Let's Talk

- Why did no one like the dog at the beginning of the story?

- Why did everyone like the dog at the end of the story?

- Have you ever thought you wouldn't like someone when you first met but then liked her a lot?

- Is it ever okay to laugh at people because they are different from you? How can you remember to treat people kindly, no matter what they look like?

- We are all special in some way. What will you do today to help someone else feel special?

Explore More

- Have children write a note or letter describing all the things they like about themselves. Let them know that no one else will see their letter, so they can write anything. Encourage them to keep the letter in their desk or on a wall at home, so they can read it during times they are not feeling good about themselves.

- Ask children to create a character who has something a little bit funny about him (maybe he has a goofy-sounding voice or a weird habit, or maybe he looks a little odd). Then have them make up a story about how his odd trait is used for something good— almost like a superhero.

- Ask: *Do you know someone who seems sad or lonely? How could you help to brighten her day? How could you let her know that you care?* If children don't mention a card, bring it up yourself and encourage them to make a picture or card and share it with that person.

Focus on Assets
26: Caring
33: Interpersonal Competence
38: Self-Esteem

Dora's Eggs
by Julie Sykes
illustrated by Jane Chapman

Dora the hen is very proud of her eggs—until she starts paying attention to the babies the *other* animals have. Why aren't her eggs fuzzy like a calf, or furry like a puppy? They don't run or snuggle either. But Dora beams with pride when her eggs finally hatch as adorable chicks.

Let's Talk

• What does it mean to be proud of something?

• Why was the hen not so proud of her eggs?

• Have you ever been really proud of yourself for something, then not so proud after comparing yourself to someone else?

• How can you remind yourself to just be proud of who you are and what you do?

Explore More

• Have children make a list of their friends and family members to prepare them for making a collage of the special people in their lives. Supply them with scissors, glue, construction paper, and old magazines and picture books so they can cut out images to use in the collage. As they're working, ask questions to spark their creative ideas, such as, *What is something that makes each of these people special? Why are you grateful for their friendship?*

• Have children think of something they are proud of and encourage them to draw a picture about it.

Focus on Assets

37: Personal Power
38: Self-Esteem

The Dot

by Peter H. Reynolds

Vashti thinks she has no artistic talents and has resigned herself to the idea that she can't draw. However, when her teacher encourages her to start by drawing just one dot and moving on from there, Vashti realizes she is capable of more than she had imagined.

Let's Talk

• Do you sing, dance, play music, draw, paint?

• Why do you think it's important to be creative like this?

• Who encourages you to do these things?

• Who can *you* encourage to be creative and do those kinds of things?

Explore More

• Use the end of the story as a writing or storytelling prompt. Have children continue the story. Ask: *What does the boy do? What does he learn? What does he draw? Does he teach something new to one of his friends? What is it?*

• Have everyone sit in a circle to make a group picture. One person should start with a simple dot or line. Proceeding clockwise, let everyone add something to the drawing.

• Variation: Do the above activity as a relay race between teams.

• Pair this with An Artist's Tale on page 131.

Focus on Assets

3: Other Adult Relationships
17: Creative Activities
38: Self-Esteem

Duck on a Bike

by David Shannon

When a duck rides a bike, the other barnyard animals aren't sure what to think. Some think he's crazy, others act jealous, and at least one, Mouse, wishes he could ride a bike too. It's not long before they all set their feelings aside to ride their own bikes all over the farm.

Let's Talk

• How did the animals react to the duck riding on his bike?

• What did they do when they got a chance to ride bikes, too?

- What is something new and fun that you tried after learning about it from someone else?

Explore More

- Invite children to pretend that farm animal toys are riding bikes or playing with other toys. If you don't have farm animals, have children play with any animal toys, or get creative and help the children make some of their own with dough or clay. After this activity, ask children why they paired certain animals with certain toys. Ask: *Which animal do you think is having the most fun? Why?*

- Give children time to write a short story about a herd of animals that find a set of toys in their yard. Ask: *How do they play with your toys? What do they think about your toys? Do you ever see them playing with the toys, or do they only play when people aren't around?*

- Ask children what they think zoo animals do at night, after the zookeeper and guests leave. Have them draw pictures of the antics.

Focus on Assets
5: Caring Neighborhood
15: Positive Peer Influence

Elmer
by David McKee

Elmer is not like the other elephants he knows—they are gray, but his body is covered in multicolored patches. Although the other elephants love his cheerfulness and sense of humor, Elmer worries that they are laughing *at* him. To make himself blend in with the other elephants, he rolls around in a pile of gray berries. Elmer soon realizes how special his real self is, and emerges more colorful than ever.

Let's Talk

- How did Elmer feel about his colors at the beginning of the book? In the middle of the book? At the end?

- How did Elmer learn to feel good about himself?

- What did Elmer's friends miss about Elmer when he was gone?

- What do you most appreciate about one of your special friends?

Explore More

- Have children sit in a circle and draw a miniature outline of themselves on a piece of construction paper. Provide them with glue and colorful little pieces of scrap paper to put inside their outline. When they are finished, instruct them to swap pictures with the person to their left and then talk to each other about their pictures. Point out that every picture will be different, but they are all special. Ask: *What do you like about your picture? What do you like about your friend's picture?*

- Have children trace an outline of their favorite animal on a large piece of paper. Give them paper scraps to make their own patchwork animal. Encourage them to give the animal a special name and put it on display.

Focus on Assets
33: Interpersonal Competence
38: Self-Esteem

Farm Flu

by Teresa Bateman, illustrated by Nadine Bernard Westcott

When a boy is left in charge of his family's farm for a day, he's in for more than he bargained for. Animal after animal comes down with the flu, and the boy resolves to take care of each one just as his mother cares for him when he is sick. When the animals start taking advantage of his kindness, however, he restricts them from TV, toys, games, and snack foods.

Let's Talk

• What do your family and friends do to make you feel better when you are sick?

• How do you take care of friends or family when they're not feeling well?

• What lessons do you think the animals learned at the end of the story?

Explore More

• After you've read the book, have the children form small groups and come up with new endings to the story.

• Use the story to talk about fiction vs. nonfiction. Show children pictures from the book, and ask them to write down everything they see that tells them this story is made up. Ask: *What are the animals doing that real animals wouldn't do?*

• Have the children act out a scene from the book.

• Have children decorate a sign that encourages people to wash their hands to avoid spreading germs.

Focus on Assets
1: Family Support
28: Integrity
29: Honesty

A Fish Out of Water

by Helen Palmer Geisel
illustrated by P. D. Eastman

When a little boy ignores directions and feeds Otto, his fish, too much food, Otto grows so big that even the bathtub and the pool are too small for him. The pet store owner comes to the rescue and restores the fish to his appropriate size.

Let's Talk

• Why did the fish grow so big?

• Would the story have been different if the boy had fed the fish the way he was supposed to? How?

• What happens when you don't follow rules?

• Why is it important to follow directions?

Explore More

• Take children on a field trip to a pet store or zoo. Prepare children with questions to ask, such as, *How do you take care of the animals? What happens if you feed the animals too much or too little? Why is it important to give the animals the right food?*

• Have the children make up their own story about a fish or some other animal that has crazy adventures. You can have the children tell the story out loud or draw it out on paper.

• Ask the children to think of a time when they weren't responsible or didn't follow directions. Have them write a story about what happened as a result.

Check out the companion book *Sam and the Firefly* by P. D. Eastman, the illustrator of *A Fish Out of Water.*

Focus on Assets
30: Responsibility

The Friend

by Sarah Stewart
illustrated by David Small

Annabelle Bernadette Clementine Dodd's parents don't have time to spend with her, so the girl's loving nanny, Bea, fills the void. The two perform daily chores together and make special trips to the beach, forging a strong bond.

Let's Talk

• Do you have a special person who helps take care of you? Who is it?

• What are some fun memories you have with this person?

• Adults who care about you often set important rules for you to follow. Why is it important to honor those rules?

• Look at the last page in the book. Who do you think the woman in the picture is? What do you think the typewriter in the picture is telling us? Is it a clue?

Explore More

• Use soft rope to gently connect partners together by one arm or one leg, so they can do "together tasks." Pairs can do jumping jacks, try to score a soccer goal, or compete in a relay race. Follow up the game with questions: *What was hard? What was easy? What does this activity teach us about being a good friend?*

• Ask children to come up with the best mom, dad, nanny, or other caring adult in the whole world. Conduct a group story circle, and have the children talk about all the wonderful things they would do with this caring adult.

• To further explore friendships through play, pair with I Like People Who Like . . ., I Know You, Friend!, or My Friend, all in the Community-Building Games section that begins on page 113.

• Have the children make a card to give a friend. Ask them to draw a picture of a memory or a picture that shows why they appreciate this special friend so much.

Focus on Assets

3: Other Adult Relationships
11: Family Boundaries
14: Adult Role Models

The Gingerbread Man

by Jim Aylesworth

In this classic fairy tale, an elderly couple bakes a gingerbread man who surprises them by popping out of the oven and running away. The bright pictures tell of the gingerbread man's adventures.

Let's Talk

• Why did the Gingerbread Man run away?

• How would *you* catch the Gingerbread Man?

• What should you do when you don't feel safe?

• What can you do to stay safe?

Explore More

• Make ornaments or door decorations in the shape of gingerbread girls and boys.

• Prepare for this activity by buying or baking gingerbread men for the children to eat when the activity is over. Let the children know that you have a special guest for them to meet after story time. Then read *The Gingerbread Man,* and tell the children you want to introduce them to the Gingerbread Man himself. Open a door or curtain to "reveal" him, and act surprised when he's not there. Ask the children to see if the Gingerbread Man is somewhere in the building. As a group, search for him while asking, *Is he here? Is he there?* Along the way, meet key people the children should know (for example, the principal, organization leader, or agency executive), and cover the building's main areas (the bathrooms, your office, the nurse's station, the kitchen/cafeteria), so they become familiar to the children. You can make the activity even more fun by creating a trail of crumbs for the children to follow (of course, check with the custodian first). After seeking out the Gingerbread Man and meeting interesting people and places along the way, return to your original room to eat gingerbread men.

Note: This activity is most effective when it is done at the beginning of the school year or program session.

• Ask children to write their own gingerbread person story. Ask: *If you baked gingerbread cookies, what adventures might your gingerbread boy or girl have?*

Focus on Assets
10: Safety
11: Family Boundaries
13: Neighborhood Boundaries

Green Eggs and Ham
by Dr. Seuss

Sam-I-am is insistent that his grown-up friend try green eggs and ham. He tries everything to make the food more appealing to the grown-up—from offering up the dish in a box, with a fox, in the rain, on a train—but the grown-up keeps refusing. When the grown-up finally gives in, he is surprised to learn that he actually likes the green eggs and ham.

Let's Talk

• Have you ever been afraid to try a new food, only to find that you liked it?

• Do you have a favorite "crazy" food to eat? What is it?

• What do you do when someone serves you a new food?

• Does this story make you more willing to try new things? Why or why not?

(IN THEIR OWN WORDS)

"One time our class ate green eggs and ham—it was yummy!"

Chad, age 8

Explore More

• Blindfold the children and have them sample a few mystery foods. Before they take off their blindfold, ask if they liked the foods or not. Then reveal what they ate.

• Dr. Seuss's birthday is March 2. Follow the lead of one school where the students and teachers dressed up for the day as their favorite Dr. Seuss character.

• Ask the children to draw a picture of the funniest thing they've ever eaten—and liked. Encourage them to make up a funny title for the picture.

• Host a funny-food lunch or picnic. Invite people to bring some of the funny foods they like best.

Focus on Assets
34: Cultural Competence

If You Give a Mouse a Cookie
by Laura Joffe Numeroff
illustrated by Felicia Bond

When a boy gives a mouse a cookie, he finds that his generosity won't stop there. The mouse starts demanding much more from the boy, and the boy exhaustedly tries to keep up with the mouse's wants and needs. The book's comical illustrations show what hap-

Third-grade teacher Peggy Saylor enjoys leading Reader's Theater with children, which gives them an opportunity to present a play, story, or poem. "When [*Green Eggs and Ham* is] presented through the medium of Reader's Theater, students are encouraged to be expressive, imaginative, and creative," she said.

pens when the mouse gets carried away with his requests.

Let's Talk

• What lessons did Mouse learn about making cookies?

• What do you like to have while you're eating cookies?

• What would happen if a mouse gave *you* a cookie?

Explore More

• Have children create their own story together. Form a circle with the children. Begin the story by filling in the blanks of this phrase, "If you give a _____ a _____, then _____ will happen." The child next to you should add on to the story, the child next to her should do the same, and so on. End by returning to the original line and allowing the story to come full circle.

• Have children use this story in Reader's Theater. Give them props and help them memorize the story line, so they can perform it for an audience.

• In call-and-response style sing the song "Who Stole the Cookie from the Cookie Jar?"

All sing: *Who stole the cookie from the cookie jar?*
Teacher: *[Child's name] stole the cookie from the cookie jar!*
Child responds: *Who, me?*
Teacher: *Yes, you!*
Child: *Couldn't be!*
Teacher: *Then who?*

Continue singing and adding new names.

Third-grade teacher Peggy Saylor suggests reading other books in the series:

• *If You Give a Moose a Muffin*

• *If You Give a Pig a Pancake*

• *If You Take a Mouse to the Movies*

• *If You Take a Mouse to School*

• *If You Give a Pig a Party*

• *If You Give a Cat a Cupcake*

Focus on Assets
32: Planning and Decision Making

I'm Gonna Like Me: Letting Off a Little Self-Esteem
by Jamie Lee Curtis
illustrated by Laura Cornell

By detailing a boy's and girl's constant self-affirmations—"I'm gonna like me 'cause I'm loved and I know it"—this dynamic story helps remind children of their good qualities and the fact that it's OK to make mistakes.

Let's Talk

• Which page was your favorite? Why?

• What's one thing you really like about yourself?

- What's one thing you really like about one of your friends?

- How can you learn to like *everything* about yourself?

Explore More

- Have children make sock puppets, and then put on a puppet show in which characters talk about the crazy and unique things they like about themselves.

- Instruct children to draw a stick figure of themselves. Then have them draw lines to various parts of their stick figure body, and write one word on each line that describes one thing they like about themselves.

- Have children create a funny list of 10 reasons they love their toes, or ears, or belly button.

- Ask children to write their own poem or story called "I'm Gonna Like Me."

Focus on Assets
1: Family Support
38: Self-Esteem

Ish

by Peter H. Reynolds

Ramon loves to draw—that is, until his brother laughs at his drawings. Disappointed and uninspired, he crumples up his artwork and vows to quit drawing. When he learns that his sister has been secretly collecting his pictures, Ramon regains hope and rediscovers his love for drawing.

Let's Talk

- Have you ever said something mean or laughed at someone else and hurt their feelings?

- Why should you look for the good things in others?

- How can you encourage others to do their best and to feel proud of their work?

- If people are nervous about their art (or soccer skills or writing), how can you help them feel more confident?

Explore More

- Pair *Ish* with An Artist's Tale. See page 131.

- Instruct children to draw a scribble on a piece of paper, and pass the paper to a friend. The friend should add to the scribble so it looks like a new picture. Have the children keep passing the picture along until several friends have contributed to the picture. Have children look at the pictures and comment on each masterpiece.

- Encourage children to keep all of their pictures, even the ones they don't like very much. Have them give the pictures their own "-ish" names, and suggest they give some of them to others as a surprise gift.

Focus on Assets
1: Family Support
17: Creative Activities
33: Interpersonal Competence

Kiss the Cow!

by Phyllis Root
illustrated by Will Hillenbrand

Annalisa's mother has a milking ritual with Luella the cow. She speaks lovingly to her, sings to her, and finishes off with a kiss on Luella's nose. Annalisa absolutely refuses to do the same. But when she finally decides to implement her mother's ritual, she follows everything *except* the kiss on the nose, and Luella stops producing milk for the family. Who knew it was so important to kiss a cow?

Let's Talk

- What does it mean to be stubborn?

- Are you ever stubborn about obeying rules at home or school?

- Have you ever missed out on something special because you were too stubborn to try?

- Why do you think it's important to follow rules?

- What should you do if you don't like a rule?

Explore More

- Instruct children to draw a picture of what their home would be like without any rules. Have them turn the page over and draw a picture of their home when people follow family rules. Ask: *Which picture makes you feel better? What rule do you need to work on in your home?*

- Ask: *Who are the people who help you every day? A neighbor? A parent? A bus driver?* Give children time to craft a thank-you note for these helpful friends by drawing a picture. Afterward, brainstorm other ways they could express their gratitude, from just saying thanks to delivering a batch of cookies or flowers.

Focus on Assets

11: Family Boundaries
12: School Boundaries
32: Planning and Decision Making

Little by Little

by Amber Stewart
illustrated by Layn Marlow

Otto the otter has many talents and skills, but there's one very important thing he can't do—swim. With support from his family and a lot of practice, he not only learns to swim, but also that he is capable and strong.

Let's Talk

- What is something you've had to learn little by little?

- What does it mean to have courage?

- Where do you find the courage to try new things?

- Who helps you learn things?

- What is something you'd like to learn to do? Who could help you?

- What is one thing that you're afraid to do that you could start to learn to do today?

Explore More

- Ask children to help you wad up several pieces of paper. Then draw six squares on the lid of a big box, and label each square with topics such as sports, forest, library, and beach. Children should take turns tossing a wad of paper onto the top of the box. When the paper lands on a square, the child should say one thing he would like to explore, study, or experience in relation to the square's topic. For example, the sports square might inspire a child to try a new sport. The beach square might remind the child that he would like to try fishing in the ocean.

- Play connect the dots. Have children sit in a circle and invite them to share something new they would like to try. If another child has a way to support her classmate in an endeavor, that child should speak up to share her ideas. Then she should share something new she would like to try. Continue until all children have had a chance to participate, and you have connected the dots between goals and resources to support those goals.

- Have children finish the following story: *I went to the zoo to visit the otters. I watched as one otter looked around to see if anyone was watching him. He swam to the side of the pool, opened a small round doorway, and went through. I decided to follow . . .*

Focus on Assets

21: Achievement Motivation
37: Personal Power
38: Self-Esteem

Long Night Moon

by Cynthia Rylant
illustrated by Mark Siegel

From January through December, each month's full moon is described through the Native American tradition of naming the moon. Beautiful illustrations enchant children while teaching them about Earth.

Let's Talk

- What do you see when you look at the moon? Do you see the man in the moon or something else?

- Which moon in the story was your favorite? Why?

- Why do you think the people in this book have so many different names for the moon?

Explore More

- Have students participate in a writing or drawing exercise. Ask the following questions to prompt their writing or illustration: *What do you think happens at night under the moon? Do the stars and the moon talk? Do animals come to play and share their day with the moon? What do they do? What do they say?*

- Encourage the children to go outside with a parent or other caring adult to see what the moon looks like on a special night, such as their birthday. Ask: *If you could name the moon this month, what name would you give it? Why?* Have them draw or write their answer.

Children's librarian Lana Settle suggests a companion book, *Barn Dance!* by Bill Martin Jr. and John Archambault, a story about a boy who likes to watch his farm by moonlight.

Focus on Assets
34: Cultural Competence

Miss Nelson Is Missi᷍

by Harry Allard
illustrated by James Marshall

After Miss Nelson's class acts defiantly, the dreaded Miss Swamp comes to get the class back into shape. The children soon miss their beloved Miss Nelson.

Let's Talk

- Why did Miss Nelson leave? Was there something else she could have done to make things better?

- Are there times you feel like being rude and not listening to adults who are in charge? What makes you feel that way?

- Why is it important to follow instructions and help others—your friends *and* adults?

Explore More

- Invite the class to make their own list of class rules and the consequences they will face if they don't follow them. Or, have the children make a list of family rules, consequences, and rewards.

- Have children create a code of honor by drawing pictures of values and behaviors that are important to them. Invite them to display the code of honor where they will be reminded to follow it.

- Play Teacher Says instead of Simon Says. See instructions on page 126.

Use *The Berenstain Bears Forget Their Manners* by Stan Berenstain as a follow-up book. Also see the sequels to this book, *Miss Nelson Is Back* and *Miss Nelson Has a Field Day.*

Focus on Assets
12: School Boundaries
30: Responsibility
35: Self-Regulation

Moe the Dog in Tropical Paradise

by Diane Stanley
illustrated by Elise Primavera

When Moe's plans for a beach vacation fall through, he and his friend transform their home into a tropical paradise.

Let's Talk

- What is a dream vacation? What would be *your* dream vacation?

- How can you make a vacation at your own house?

- How do you respond when you don't get what you want or things don't go the way you want them to? How could you find a way to make the best of the situation?

Explore More

- Say: *Think of a place where you've always wanted to go. Pretend that you are going to transform your bedroom into that special place. Draw a picture of what your bedroom would look like if you turned it into your "dream vacation."*

- Have children write a story about what they would do and see on their own dream vacation.

- Let children build their own sand castles with real sand.

Focus on Assets

32: Planning and Decision Making

Mole Music

by David McPhail

Mole becomes inspired when he hears a man playing the most beautiful violin music on TV. He buys his own violin, and every night, after a day full of digging, begins practicing. As time goes on, Mole's music becomes so beautiful that it nurtures the growth of an oak tree.

Let's Talk

- What kinds of music do you like best?

- What instruments would you like to play? Do you think you could learn to play an instrument like Mole did?

- Have you ever worked as hard as Mole did on something you like, such as music, or sports, or memorizing something? What was it?

Explore More

- Find kazoos, recorders, and harmonicas, and teach the children simple songs. At the end of the week, have them perform for you, in either small groups or one large group.

- Do the Human Band activity on page 130.

- Let children use odds and ends such as boxes, cans, or spoons to make their own instruments. Then have them practice so they can perform for the group or family and friends.

- Do the Clang Clang activity on page 134. Then have the children use all the noise-makers to make their own music.

Focus on Assets

16: High Expectations
17: Creative Activities
21: Achievement Motivation
39: Sense of Purpose

Not a Stick
by Antoinette Portis

A pig demonstrates that a stick isn't just a stick: it becomes whatever the pig imagines it to be, whether it's a sword to fight dragons, a fishing rod, a baton, or a paintbrush.

Let's Talk

- Which "not a stick" picture is your favorite? Why?

- What else could the stick be?

- Have you ever made anything neat and fun out of a stick? What did you make?

- What helps you think of fun new ways to play, like the character in *Not a Stick*?

Explore More

- Put a stick in the middle of the room. Ask the children: *What could the stick be today? What if you were in a forest—what might the stick be? What if you were in an ocean? What if you were in the desert? What if you were in your bedroom?*

- Draw a triangle on a whiteboard or big piece of paper. Ask: *When is a triangle not a triangle?* Then have children draw as many pictures as they can, using the triangle as part of the base. Continue to explore with other shapes, such as a fork, a rock, or a swirl. Do this exploration as a conversation, or challenge children to pick one shape and create their own "Not a . . ." book.

If you like this book, read *Not a Box,* also by Antoinette Portis.

Focus on Assets
9: Service to Others
30: Responsibility
32: Planning and Decision Making

The Other Side
by Jacqueline Woodson
illustrated by E. B. Lewis

Clover is a young Black girl whose mother has instructed her never to climb the fence that keeps Blacks and Whites in her town apart. Annie is a White girl who has received the same instructions from her own mother. Over time, the two girls get to know each other from opposite sides of the fence and finally decide that they should both sit atop the fence. Neither one has officially broken the rules, but together they have broken down barriers.

Let's Talk

- Why did the families want the girls to stay apart and keep to their own sides of the fence?

- Do you have any friends that are a little different from you?

- In the end, were the girls so different after all? Why or why not?

Explore More

- Draw a fence on a whiteboard or big piece of paper and ask the children if a fence has ever kept them apart from another person. Have them draw their own fence and add a gate to it. Then have them write about ways they can overcome differences to be friends with anyone. Ask: *How can you see past people's differences to be friends?*

- Play Hot Potato Toss, What Makes Me "Me," or Human Bingo in the games section to further explore friendships, common traits, and what makes each of us unique. See pages 113 and 117.

Focus on Assets
28: Integrity
33: Interpersonal Competence
34: Cultural Competence

Put Me in the Zoo
by Robert Lopshire

This classic book is about a colorfully spotted leopard who desperately wants to live in the zoo. After the leopard shows his friends all the tricks he can do with colorful spots, they help him find a perfect place to use his talents.

Let's Talk

• What kinds of tricks could the leopard do?

• What tricks can you do?

• How can you use your talents, the things you do well, to help others?

Explore More

• Ask children to make a list of animals in the zoo and in the circus. Ask: *Which animal is your favorite? Why? What can that animal do that makes it special?*

• Have a show-and-tell time in which all the children in the group demonstrate their own skills and talents. People might share a gymnastic trick, the ability to curl their tongue, or how to sing a song. Emphasize that everyone has skills to share.

• Have children make a picture out of colorful dots of all shapes and sizes. Hang their pictures somewhere prominent.

Focus on Assets
38: Self-Esteem
39: Sense of Purpose
40: Positive View of Personal Future

A Quiet Place
by Douglas Wood
illustrated by Dan Andreasen

A boy searches high and low for a retreat from the noises and distractions of the city. He tries the woods, the beach, the desert, the top of a hill, even the museum and library, but where he finally finds a quiet place is within himself.

Let's Talk

• What is your favorite quiet place to go?

• Why is it important for everyone to have a little bit of quiet time?

• What would you dream about in your quiet place?

• Who would you invite to share some time with you in your quiet place? Why?

Explore More

• Challenge children to use each letter of the alphabet and think of a place they could go for quiet time that starts with each letter. (For example, B: bedroom, F: friend's house, L: library)

• Play Quiet Mouse, Still Mouse, letting children compete to see who can be the quietest and stillest. The winner gets to be the leader for the next round.

• When you're done reading the book, ask children to imagine themselves as part of the story.

Focus on Assets
20: Time at Home
39: Sense of Purpose

THE EXPERTS WEIGH IN

"This book is excellent for stirring imagination in children," says children's librarian Lana Settle. "The little boy in the book has many quiet places to visit. In each one, his imagination runs wild as he pretends to be a character in a different place or time."

Something Might Happen

by Helen Lester
illustrated by Lynn Munsinger

Twitchly Fidget is a lemur with a problem—he's afraid of everything, even washing his fur and putting on his shoes. He's sure something bad will happen, so he keeps to himself and refuses to leave his house. When his aunt finally comes to visit, she proves that his fears are baseless by washing his fur and putting on his shoes—with no repercussions at all. He gains the courage to leave the house and take part in life.

Let's Talk

• What was Twitchly afraid of?

• What helped Twitchly get over his fears?

• What is something you are afraid of?

• What might help you be brave?

Explore More

• Ask children to draw pictures of themselves being brave and overcoming something they're afraid of.

• Have children write down their worries on a piece of paper and toss them to the "wind." (Have them throw their paper in the air and watch while it flutters down to the floor.) Collect the papers, and without identifying any children, read aloud a few worries. Ask the whole group what helps them feel better about each particular worry. Draw a line through each worry, and write at least one positive suggestion next to it. Let the children know that they can get their paper back to take home later and that the positive suggestions will help them carry home hope instead of worry.

• Start by naming a fear you have, and then ask the children to write down a fear of their own. Have the students put their fears in a big hat, and then draw out one piece of paper at a time. Talk about each fear as a group. Brainstorm how that fear can be faced and overcome. After talking about what helps the children conquer their fears, give them a piece of yarn to tie around their finger as a reminder that they can overcome their fears, and that they have recognized something or someone who can help them.

Pair this book with *Wemberly Worried* by Kevin Henkes.

Focus on Assets
1: Family Support
37: Personal Power
40: Positive View of Personal Future

Stellaluna

by Janell Cannon

After Stellaluna, a baby bat, is attacked by an owl and separated from her mother, a family of birds takes her in. She tries her best to fit in, but has a difficult time. When she learns to fly, she is able to find her own mother, who assures Stellaluna that it's OK for her to hang upside down and sleep at night, just as her instincts have told her.

Let's Talk

• How are you and your friends the same? How are you different?

• How can you remember to be happy with yourself, even if you are different from others?

• How do having things in common and liking the same things help build strong friendships?

• How do differences among people help build strong friendships?

Explore More

- Teach the children how to make a papier-mâché bat or bird. Prepare by tearing newspaper into two-inch-wide strips. Then crunch up newspaper in your hands and mold it into the shape of a bat or bird. Wrap masking tape around it. In a medium-sized bowl, mix one part water-based glue (such as Elmer's) with one part water. Dip strips of newspaper in the mixture, covering each piece thoroughly, and run each piece through your fingers to remove any excess paste before adding the strips to the wad that is held together with masking tape. Let the birds and bats dry overnight; then, decorate with acrylic paint.

- Encourage children to name their bird or bat, and ask: *What adventures might your bird or bat take during the day?*

- Ask the children to pretend that they were raised by a group of animals (a herd of cows, a pack of wolves, a family of raccoons). Ask: *How would your life have been different? What would you have learned about yourself?*

- Have the children create bat journals. Learn about bats together, and in the journal, answer questions such as, *What do they look like? What do they eat? Where do they live? When do they sleep?*

Check out the companion book *The Jungle Book* by Rudyard Kipling.

Focus on Assets
33: Interpersonal Competence
34: Cultural Competence

Sunflower House
by Eve Bunting
illustrated by Kathryn Hewitt

A little boy plants a circle of sunflowers that grow so large they are able to shelter him and his friends like a house all summer. The children are catapulted into a world of imagination until the flowers begin to die. The boy and his friends have hope, however. They gather some seeds to eat and leave the rest in the ground, so these seeds can bloom and once again create beautiful flowers.

Let's Talk

- What was your favorite way that the children used the circle of sunflowers?

- Have you ever planted something and watched it grow? How did it make you feel?

- What lesson did the children learn from the sunflowers dying?

Explore More

- Have children draw their own circle of flowers and write a story about what they imagine lives among the flowers. You can adapt this activity to other seasons by using a circle of leaves, a patch of pumpkins, and so on.

- Ask: *Do you ever pick dandelions and blow the seeds off? Where do you think the seeds go? Write a story about the many places dandelions travel.*

- If you have the opportunity to go outdoors, find a nearby circle of trees and play in it for a while. Say: *Who could live here? What do they eat? What do they do for fun? Where do they sleep?*

Focus on Assets
17: Creative Activities
33: Interpersonal Competence

Those Can-Do Pigs
by David McPhail

The can-do pigs really can do a lot. They can fly, fend off sharks, charm snakes, and even tickle generals so convincingly that they agree to stop waging wars.

Let's Talk

• What is your favorite thing that the can-do pigs did? Why is that your favorite?

• What is something that you *can* do, even when some people think you can't?

Explore More

• Engage the children in rhyming competitions. First, give them one minute to write down all the words they can think of that rhyme with a simple given word (*pig, cow, dog*). Then allow them another minute to make up silly words that rhyme with the word you've given. To go further, have them write a short poem that uses a mix of the real and silly words.

• Ask the children to think up their own animals that are good at doing things, and then have them share the crazy things the animals can do.

• Ask the children: *What is something you've always wanted to do? Write about how you can do it.*

• Play Rhymes Scramble on page 120.

For a double dose of confidence building, pair with *The Little Engine That Could* by Watty Piper.

Focus on Assets
37: Personal Power
38: Self-Esteem
39: Sense of Purpose
40: Positive View of Personal Future

Today I Feel Silly and Other Moods That Make My Day
by Jamie Lee Curtis
illustrated by Laura Cornell

This vibrant book follows the many different moods a little girl goes through in one day—silly, grumpy and mean, excited, confused—and lets kids know that all feelings are OK to have *and* express.

Let's Talk

• How are you feeling today?

• What do you do when you feel silly? What about when you are full of energy?

• What do you do when you feel scared? What about when you feel sad?

• Who are some adults in your life who love you no matter what mood you are in?

• How can you help your friends when they are feeling sad or having a bad day?

Explore More

• Give children time to explore their silly sides. They can do anything, within reason. Let them make silly expressions, draw or paint silly faces, wear silly costumes, or write silly stories.

• Have children make masks to represent their different moods. Make them with cut-out paper or papier-mâché.

• Make paper-plate masks. Have children trace and cut out holes for eyes, decorate eyelashes with glitter, and make features using markers. Then use a hole punch on each side of the plate to tie yarn through, creating a strap to go around the back of the child's head.

• Have children create their own play about the silliest things ever.

- Try the following writing prompts: *Today I feel . . .* or *When I'm feeling [sad, scared, shy], my [mom, dad, favorite book, teddy bear] helps me to feel [happy, brave, confident].*

- Form a story circle. Have children take turns sharing the silly things they've done or seen by saying "The silliest thing I've ever done is . . ." or "The silliest thing I've ever seen is . . ."

Focus on Assets
38: Self-Esteem

Tom's Tail

by Linda M. Jennings
illustrated by Tim Warnes

Tom the pig complains so much about his curly tail that the other barnyard animals are determined to help him change it. They finally transform it by pulling the tail straight, caking it with mud, and letting it dry. Tom is delighted until he realizes that his new pointy tail pokes his friends. When a rainfall comes along and washes the mud away, Tom decides to stick with his curly tail after all.

Let's Talk

- Why didn't Tom want to have a curly tail?

- What changed his mind?

- Talk about a time when you wanted something, got it, and then realized you didn't really want it.

- Why is it important to like ourselves just the way we are?

Explore More

- Play the "Mirror" game. Have children pair up with a friend and carefully copy everything the friend says or does. Ask: *What would the world be like if everyone was the same?*

- Play What Makes Me "Me," Human Bingo, or Hot Potato Toss to explore ways people are alike and different. See the games section on pages 113 and 117 for instructions.

- Host a robot day. Send a note to parents that explains the idea: on a specified day, you would like all of the children to wear the same color clothes, so they can pretend to be robots. Make sure to mention the color you would like the children to wear. Keep the rules loose to leave room for families who may not have many clothes to choose from, and be sensitive to cultural differences. If the children show up on robot day and they aren't all wearing the same color clothes, minimize the event so no one feels left out. If you decide to go ahead full force, have children speak like robots. Act distressed, as though you can't tell the "robots" apart, and then talk about how grateful you are that the children are actually unique and different from each other.

Focus on Assets
38: Self-Esteem

Tuesday

by David Wiesner

On this particular Tuesday, some plump frogs embark on an adventure, taking off on lily pads that float and hover like magic carpets. They take off from their swamp and journey over the countryside and through a town, all the while playing tricks on everyone from unsuspecting birds in flight to a grandma who's dozing off in front of the TV. The illustrations in this book do most of the work, as virtually no words are used.

Let's Talk

- Which part of the book did you like best? Why?

- What are some animals that really can fly?

- If you could fly, where would you want to go? What do you think you would see?

Explore More

- Use recycled paper to have children make their own jumping frog. Find instructions at www.wikihow.com/Make-an-Origami-Jumping-Frog.

- Hold story time. Have children take turns telling their own story to go with the pictures from *Tuesday*.

- Have the children draw pictures of all the animals they can think of that fly. Ask: *Which one do you like best? Which animal would you like to be?*

Focus on Assets
17: Creative Activities

The Turn-Around, Upside-Down Alphabet Book

by Lisa Campbell Ernst

Each page contains a letter that can transform into an animal, a food, or a nature scene when the reader turns the book every which way. A *J* becomes an elephant's trunk, an *O* turns into a fried egg, a *W* becomes a mountain stream. The book is much like watching for shapes in the clouds.

Let's Talk

- Which picture was your favorite? Why?

- If you could have made a picture from one of the letters in the book, what would you have made?

- What would the book have been like if the author had made pictures from shapes like triangles, circles, and squares? What pictures might you have seen then?

Explore More

- Give the group one letter (e.g., *O*) to make as many pictures as they can within one minute. Let children share their pictures and celebrate their creative imaginations. A variation is to have children create a collage of pictures using the letters of their first name. To take the activity further, have them create a story using all the pictures they drew based on their name.

- Have children pair up and write the letters of the alphabet on one piece of paper at a time. Instruct them to turn the pages around and around to see what new pictures they can find.

- Play Alphabet Pictures. See page 132 in the Artsy Games section of this book.

Focus on Assets
17: Creative Activities
22: School Engagement

Walking through the Jungle

by Julie Lacome

Rhymes, imagination, adventure, and hidden animals make this colorful book a delightful read.

Let's Talk

• What was your favorite animal surprise?

• Have you ever found animals hiding outside? What were they? What happened when you found them?

• How many animals do you think we could find outside if we used binoculars or a magnifying glass? Where would we find them?

Explore More

• Play I Spy. The leader says, "I spy something yellow. Can you find it?" Then, the other children try to find what the leader is thinking about. The person who guesses correctly becomes the next leader.

• Use the game Spy Masters or puzzle books and games by Usborne to bring the story to life. For Spy Masters directions, see page 135 of the games section.

• Choose a page from *Walking through the Jungle* and have children look at it carefully. Then close the book and give children one minute to try to write down everything they saw in the picture. Try this activity with a few different jungle pages, and see if it becomes easier for children each time.

• If you have the opportunity to go outside, sit together at a park to watch for animals, birds, and insects. Have the children draw or write down all the creatures they see.

Focus on Assets

17: Creative Activities

Wemberly Worried

by Kevin Henkes

Wemberly the mouse worries about everything—her parents' well-being, her stuffed rabbit Petal, the equipment at the jungle gym, whether she'll fit in with other kids—but when she goes off to nursery school, she meets Jewel, a perfect match who helps Wemberly worry a little bit less.

Let's Talk

• What are some things that frighten Wemberly?

• Should any of those things really scare us? Why or why not?

• What frightens you?

• What do you do when you're afraid?

• Who helps you be brave and feel less afraid?

Explore More

• Play the "What If" game. Have children sit in a circle. Ask them to imagine that they are going on a trip into outer space. Going around the circle, ask each child to share a "what if." Before you start, give an example for children to follow, such as "What if we run out of astronaut ice cream?" After everyone has expressed a "what if," talk about ways to ease worries in everyday life.

• Provide old shoe boxes (or have children bring one in) for the children to create a "worry box." Beforehand, cut a slot into the top of each box, and then have the children decorate the box with positive images (smiley faces, puppies, rainbows) and phrases such as "Go away, worries!" Tell them that when they're worried, they should write down their worries and put them in the box—it will hold their worries so they don't have to.

For more books and activities that deal with worry, see:

- *Something Might Happen* by Helen Lester, page 77.

- *A Bad Case of Stripes* by David Shannon, page 60.

Focus on Assets
37: Personal Power
38: Self-Esteem

When Sophie Gets Angry—Really, Really Angry

by Molly Bang

When Sophie's sister grabs Sophie's stuffed gorilla from her, Sophie gets so angry that she throws a tantrum and runs off into the woods by herself. She finds comfort by climbing a beech tree, from which she can gaze at the water and feel soothed. She is able to return to her family with a calmer outlook.

Let's Talk

- What do you do when you're really, really mad?

- What are some good ways to make yourself less angry?

- Is it ever OK for you to run off by yourself without telling your parents or teachers where you are going? (After some discussion, say: *It's OK to try to make yourself less angry, but the adults who care about you also want to make sure you're safe and help you get over whatever made you mad.*)

Explore More

- Role-play situations that might make kids angry, and let the children express both healthy and inappropriate responses to the anger. A variation is to make this a freeze-tag role play. Have two people start the role play. When someone else wants to join, he should yell "Freeze!" and tag the person he wants to replace.

- Have children practice various techniques for dealing with anger, such as counting to 10; breathing in deeply for an eight count, holding breath for a seven count, then letting it out for an eight count; doing something physical, such as jumping jacks or taking a short walk; and laughing out loud (even if they don't feel like it). After each technique, ask them how they feel. Ask: *Which one would you use when you're really angry? Why?*

- Ask: *What is something you sometimes do that makes another person angry? Is it a kind thing to do? How can you remember to be kind in the future?*

- Have the children draw a picture of themselves doing something that makes them feel less angry.

Focus on Assets
35: Self-Regulation

Wilfrid Gordon McDonald Partridge

by Mem Fox
illustrated by Julie Vivas

Wilfrid Gordon McDonald Partridge isn't the only person with so many names—Nancy Alison Delacourt Cooper has four names, too, and Wilfrid loves to talk with her and the other elderly residents at the home next door. Together, they share memories, giving each other reasons to smile.

Let's Talk

- Why did the little boy want to help his elderly friend remember things?

- What are some special times that you remember?

- What special memories do you have with adults in your life, like your grandma, grandpa, uncle, or aunt?

Explore More

- Have the children sit in a circle to play Memory Word. Ask them a starter question, such as "What does spring remind you of?" If the first child says, "Spring reminds me of baseball," the next child would say, "Baseball reminds me of running," then "Running reminds me of the beach," "The beach reminds me of seashells," and so on. Continue until you've gone around the entire circle.

- Invite an elderly person to come talk to the children. Prior to the visit, have children play Cub Reporter (see page 116) with a partner to build their interviewing skills. Have children ask the visitor questions they've come up with after reading *Wilfrid Gordon McDonald Partridge*. You could also ask your guest to read the book aloud to the children.

- Ask the children to draw pictures or write stories about their best memories.

Focus on Assets
3: Other Adult Relationships

Willy the Dreamer
by Anthony Browne

Willy the chimp has big dreams. He stars in movies, sings like Elvis, and dances in a ballet, all from the comfort of his armchair. Carefully hidden bananas add some excitement to this already whimsical book.

Let's Talk

- Which dream was your favorite? Why?

- What do you dream of being or doing when you grow up?

Explore More

- Using the directions on page 105, have children make their own picture book of things they want to do when they grow up.

- Have students work in pairs with the two pictures of Willy dreaming on the chair. Ask them to work together to find the differences between the two pictures.

- Tell the children the careers you thought of having when you were their age, and how you decided on the job you have. Ask them what they think they might want to be when they grow up.

Focus on Assets
39: Sense of Purpose
40: Positive View of Personal Future

THE EXPERTS WEIGH IN

Lana Settle, a children's librarian, likes to ask her students to notice the bananas on each page and then follows up with her own activity. She tells her students, "See how the illustrator has created pictures with the bananas? Choose a different fruit or vegetable and create your own picture ideas with it."

Alexander and the Terrible, Horrible, No Good, Very Bad Day

by Judith Viorst
illustrated by Ray Cruz

Alexander's day starts out horribly and doesn't get much better as it goes on—from gum in his hair to tripping over a skateboard to discovering a cavity, he just can't catch a break. He considers moving to Australia, but in the end, Alexander realizes he's not the only one who has bad days, and there are good days ahead.

Let's Talk

• What's the best way you can think of to turn a bad day into a good day?

• Why do you think it's important to have fun and be able to laugh when things go wrong?

• What different ways do you feel at different times? How do you show your feelings in healthy and good ways?

Explore More

• Have children write or tell a new story called "Alexander and the Fantastic, Wonderful, Super-Great Day."

• Create a mood meter by having children draw faces with different expressions that show the whole range of emotions they might feel in any given day. Hang the meter on the wall and add a tack and an arrow, so children can use the mood meter to mark how they feel.

• Give the children old clothes or costumes to dress up in, and have them perform *Alexander and the Terrible, Horrible, No Good, Very Bad Day.*

Focus on Assets
35: Self-Regulation

THE EXPERTS WEIGH IN

"This book helps children deal with frustration and disappointment in a fun way. We read this a lot on bad days!"
Dianne Harper, tutoring and educational specialist and mother

Appelemando's Dreams

by Patricia Polacco

When Appelemando dreams, his friends can actually see what he is imagining in bright, vivid colors, a welcome phenomenon in their drab village. Before long they realize that his dreams stick to moist objects, which is played out beautifully on a rainy day. Appelemando's dreams serve to transform his village into a brighter, more accepting, and more loving community.

Let's Talk

• If Appelemando's friends hadn't encouraged him to dream, what might have happened? Would they have been found?

• Have you ever had a really fun dream? What was it?

• What would you do if someone tried to stop you from dreaming?

• How can you help adults play? Do you share your dreams with caring adults? What do they think of your dreams?

Explore More

• Ask: *If you could rewrite this story, how would you change it?* Have the children share their thoughts out loud, by telling a story, or through a picture.

- Instruct children to write about a time they encouraged a friend to pursue her interests or dreams.

- Encourage children to pay attention to the dreams they have while they're sleeping, and ask them to draw a picture of one they remember.

Focus on Assets

3: Other Adult Relationships
4: Caring Neighborhood
16: High Expectations

Babushka Baba Yaga

by Patricia Polacco

Knowing that people believe her to be an evil witch, Baba Yaga hides her pointy, elflike ears and wears human clothing in order to be regarded as "normal" and as a suitable caretaker for a young boy named Victor. When the other old women tell Victor terrifying stories of the "witch" Baba Yaga, she retreats to her home in the woods, only to be followed by a lonely Victor, who faces a pack of angry wolves. Baba Yaga saves the boy and her horrible reputation.

Let's Talk

- Why was Baba Yaga sad at the beginning of the story?

- What did the community think of Baba Yaga?

- How would you describe who she really is?

- What changed the way people saw her?

Explore More

- Bring in three apples—one red, one yellow, and one green. Ask the children what they think the center of each apple will look like. Will each be as different as the outside, or the same? Cut each apple in half and note that each halved core has the same bright star. Talk to the children about the importance of not judging others based on their appearance. Pass out an outline of an apple and ask the children to label what they think is at the "core" of their own heart and character. Have the group talk about core values and how they can help us learn to get along, accept each other, and take pride in who we are.

- Share with the children a time when you judged someone by his appearance instead of getting to know him first. Now ask the children to write a story about a time they did the same. When they've finished writing their stories, ask them to describe how they will respond the next time they are tempted to judge someone by her appearance.

- Encourage the children to write a thank-you note to a grandparent or older friend who has helped take care of them. Help them get started on the note by asking them why they appreciate and respect this person.

Focus on Assets

26: Caring
33: Interpersonal Competence

Book! Book! Book!

by Deborah Bruss
illustrated by Tiphanie Beeke

The barnyard animals find themselves with little to do after the children have gone back to school, so they go to the library to find some entertainment. They run into a problem, however, when the librarian can't understand the horse's neighs or the cow's moos. It isn't until a hen says "Book! Book!" that she realizes the animals want to hold a story hour back on the farm.

Let's Talk

• Why did the animals get bored?

• What did they do to try to enjoy themselves?

• What do you do when you get bored?

• What are your favorite things to do during your free time?

Explore More

• Host a book party. Have children bring their favorite book and then read it with a classmate. Or, collaborate with another teacher, so your students can read a book to younger children who haven't yet learned to read.

• Have the children work with a partner to make a list of fun things to do when they're feeling bored at home. When they're home, they can put each idea on a slip of paper, place the papers in a bucket or hat, and draw a piece of paper whenever they're looking for something fun to do.

Focus on Assets

17: Creative Activities
20: Time at Home
25: Reading for Pleasure

A Chair for My Mother

by Vera B. Williams

After her family loses their home in a fire, a little girl begins saving coins with her mother and grandmother so they can buy a big, soft chair to relax in. Every night after working at the Blue Tile Diner, the mother adds her tips to the jar, and soon the trio is on their way to pick out a new chair, with Grandma feeling like Goldilocks and mother and daughter basing their choice on how well they'll be able to cuddle up together.

Let's Talk

• When you get money to keep for yourself, what do you like to do with it?

• Have you ever saved up your money to buy something special? What is something you would like to save up money for?

• Have you ever helped a friend or neighbor who needed help like this family did? How did it feel to help?

Explore More

• Invite an agency to come in and share some of the needs people have during hard times. Ask the children if they would like to collect items for one to two weeks to give to the agency. Let them brainstorm what the items should be (for example, hats and gloves during the winter). **Note:** Use discretion when carrying out this activity, as there may be children in your class or in your care whose families have similar needs and use these services.

• Ask: *Can you think of someone who has had a hard time lately—maybe someone who has been very sick or has had a fire in his home? How could you help this person during such a hard time? Do you think any of your friends might want to help out, too?*

• Explain to the children that one of the hard things about losing everything is losing mementos like family photos or a child's drawing. Tell children that they can help make new mementos for a family by decorating a plate, making table place mats (using colored paper, stickers, markers or crayons, and lamination), or a holiday decoration.

- Have the children make a bank out of a box, canister, or carton and decorate it. Ask them to think about something they would like to save money for. Then have them write it on a slip of paper and deposit it in their new bank. Suggest that they put the bank in a special place so they'll remember to save money toward their goal.

Focus on Assets

1: Family Support
26: Caring
32: Planning and Decision Making

Clorinda

by Robert Kinerk
illustrated by Steven Kellogg

Clorinda the cow dreams of being a dancer in Manhattan, so she practices and practices in order to succeed. After giving it her best shot, she discovers that dancing, for her, is best done at home.

Let's Talk

- Have you ever tried to do something, even when people told you that you couldn't do it?

- Have you ever practiced really hard to do something? What was it?

- What is something you have never tried but would really like to? What keeps you from trying? What would help you decide to give it a try?

Explore More

- Read the story again and ask questions throughout, such as *What is the good news of*

this story? What is the bad news of this story? Have the children come up with a story that contains both good and bad news. Ask: *What should the good news be? How about the bad news?* Encourage the children to watch for the "silver lining" in any bad things that happen this week.

- Read aloud a portion of Martin Luther King Jr.'s "I Have a Dream" speech. Challenge the children to finish the speech with their own thoughts and hopes. Post the new speeches around the room or in the hallway for others to see.

- Read a story about someone who has achieved one of her dreams. Have the children talk about the things that helped this person reach her goal and how it must have felt when this person accomplished her dream. Have children make a list of the things that will help them achieve their own dreams, and encourage them to post the list by their desk or cubby, in their bedroom, or on the refrigerator at home.

- Ask the children to think about their dreams and goals, and what they can do to reach those dreams. Have them write down their dreams and their ideas for achieving them.

Focus on Assets

17: Creative Activities
37: Personal Power
40: Positive View of Personal Future

Cloudy with a Chance of Meatballs

by Judi Barrett
illustrated by Ron Barrett

The residents of Chewandswallow get their three squares a day from the clouds, not the grocery store. At mealtime, the sky opens up and sends soup, juice, mashed potatoes—whatever the meal calls for. Things get ugly, however, when the weather goes south and the food grows so large that the people of Chewandswallow have to act fast and work together to save their town—and each other.

Let's Talk

- What part of the book did you think was fun?

- How did the people of the town work together?

- What else could they have done to save the town?

Explore More

- Have children write their own food poem with funny rhythms and rhymes.

- Ask the children if they know what a pun is. If they seem to understand the idea of a pun, have them write and tell their own jokes using word puns.

- Check the weather in your area for the upcoming week. Then have children make up a story about what wacky weather might come with the real weather.

Focus on Assets

7: Community Values Children

THE EXPERTS WEIGH IN

"Silly and fun—great jumping-off point for journaling or creative writing."

Amy Anderson, teacher, owner of Let's Explore, mother of two

Danny and the Dinosaur
by Syd Hoff

Danny is able to realize a great dream when he visits the museum and a dinosaur comes to life to share in the adventures of Danny's day. They go everywhere and do everything together. They eat ice cream, attend a ball game, and play hide-and-seek with Danny's friends, until the magical day comes to an end and the dinosaur returns to the museum and Danny to his normal life.

Let's Talk

- Have you ever visited a museum? What kind of museum?

- What have you learned about dinosaurs? What would you like to learn about dinosaurs?

- If the story had a dragon in it instead of a dinosaur, how would the story have been different?

- What animals would you like to ride? Why?

Explore More

- Ask children to choose their favorite dinosaur and write their own story about spending a day together in a city with that dinosaur.

- Ask the children to think about all the different animals in a zoo. Use the following questions to prompt them to write a story they can share with the class or their friends: *If you could talk to one animal and hang out with it for a day, where would you go? What would you talk about? What would you do?*

- Play Animal Charades on page 132.

- Take children to the library and find more books about dinosaurs. Ask them to find out what dinosaurs eat, where they sleep, and how they spend their days.

Focus on Assets

17: Creative Activities
26: Caring
33: Interpersonal Competence

Flat Stanley
by Jeff Brown and Scott Nash

Stanley is shocked to find that his body has been flattened by a bulletin board, but soon he discovers that being flat can work to his advantage.

Let's Talk

• What happened to Stanley?

• How did he use his flatness in a good way?

• How did Stanley work together with his friends and family to keep doing things even though he was flat?

Explore More

• Explain to children that we are all heroes in our own way, even if we aren't Flat Stanley or Superman. A person might be a hero just because she loves to read and always works hard at school. Have children create their own "everyday superhero" image. Ask them to come to school the next day as that superhero wearing anything, such as sunglasses, a hat, or even a towel as a cape.

• Emphasize that heroes come in all colors, shapes, and sizes. They include people like the parent who works two jobs so a child can go to school, or the child who always sticks up for the underdog. Ask children to write a story about one of their everyday heroes—not someone famous, but someone in their life who is a good person and always tries to do the right thing. Or, instruct children to draw a picture or sculpt a clay figure of their hero and name an award they'd like to give to this person.

• Describe a scenario for children to act out that lets them be a hero. For example, someone is new at school or in the neighborhood—how can they be a hero to that person?

• Make flat versions of the children. Have children lie on a large piece of butcher paper and trace their body with a pencil. Inside their body's outline, they can write or draw adventures they might have if they were flattened.

• Play the Superhero Team Relay on page 136 or Superheroes Live and in Action! on page 129.

Focus on Assets
37: Personal Power
39: Sense of Purpose

THE EXPERTS WEIGH IN

"My son's class created a flat Nicholas—or whatever each child's name was—and mailed it to a pen pal with instructions from the teacher to take pictures and share interesting information about their geographical regions, then send flat Nicholas back to school. When the kids shared their flat Nicholas with the class, everyone got to learn about different geographical areas, different customs around the country, and different lifestyles. In addition, the kids got to learn how to write a proper letter, address an envelope, and 'talk' with someone through a letter."

Marci McClain, teacher and mother

Freckle Juice

by Judy Blume

Andrew wishes he had as many freckles as his classmate Nicky—in fact, he wants freckles so badly that he pays another classmate, Sharon, for her freckle juice recipe, a surefire blend of ingredients that will make his dreams come true.

Let's Talk

- Have you ever wanted something that wasn't yours? What was it?

- What can you do to be happy with what you have instead of wanting what someone else has?

- What is something you would like to change about yourself that *is* doable if you eat good food, practice a lot, or ask for help when you need it?

- What is the difference between things you want in order to improve your life and things you want just because someone else has them?

Explore More

- Change the story. Ask: *What could the boy want instead of freckles? How should he go about getting it?*

- Have children create a self-portrait with crayons, pencils, or charcoal.

- Have children trace one of their hands on a piece of construction paper. Then, on each drawn finger, have them write one special thing about themselves that makes them proud. Hang the handprints in the classroom to remind the children of their unique traits.

Focus on Assets

37: Personal Power
38: Self-Esteem
40: Positive View of Personal Future

The Great Fuzz Frenzy

by Susan Stevens Crummel
illustrated by Janet Stevens

The story starts out innocently enough when some prairie dogs find a tennis ball and begin to accessorize with pieces of fuzz they've plucked from it. But word soon spreads to prairie dogs near and far, and it isn't long before the tennis ball is completely fuzz-free. The situation soon results in a war that is finally resolved when the prairie dogs must all band together to save one of their own from a greater threat.

Let's Talk

- How did the prairie dogs act when they saw the fuzz in their den?

- What would have been a smarter way to react?

- Next time you notice that you and your friends are being selfish like the prairie dogs, what could you do to stop being so selfish?

Explore More

- Have children write their own silly story. Ask: *What can you do with a ball of fuzz?*

- Hold a tennis ball up in front of the class. Ask the children to think about what it looks like besides a tennis ball. Have them form teams of two or three and take turns telling each other the silly adventures the tennis ball might have. Give them idea prompts. Say: *Your tennis ball might go to the fair, the store, the park, school, or someplace that is special to you.*

Focus on Assets

26: Caring
33: Interpersonal Competence
36: Peaceful Conflict Resolution

The Hallo-Wiener

by Dav Pilkey

Oscar is a wiener dog who is sick and tired of being made fun of for his odd shape—short and extremely long. He hopes to turn things around by wearing a scary costume for Halloween, but his mother has something else in mind—a hot dog bun costume. Oscar is disappointed, but he heads out to trick-or-treat with his friends anyway, trailing along in his clumsy outfit as they rush ahead to get the best treats. But Oscar saves the day when he rescues his friends from a "monster"—two cats in one costume—who chases them into a lake.

Let's Talk

• What did Oscar show by helping the dogs who used to make fun of him?

• Have you ever been teased? How did it make you feel? How did you react?

• What's the right way to treat people who are different from you?

• How can we do the right thing when people are unkind to us?

Explore More

• Ask children to create their own picture of the monster that scared the dogs. Have them use noodles, candies, beans, or other supplies to make their monster. Then have them write a story to accompany their picture.

• Have wiener dogs for lunch. Use a hot dog for the body, pieces of bread for the head and legs, and dots of ketchup and mustard for the eyes, mouth, feet, and tail.

• Make monster mush. Have children each bring in a small bag of their favorite snack food or cereal. Then let children mix and match the various treats to make monster mush. As they are eating their monster mush, tell a story about all the dogs sharing monster mush after their monster scare.

Focus on Assets

26: Caring
28: Integrity
33: Interpersonal Competence
36: Peaceful Conflict Resolution

How to Make an Apple Pie and See the World

by Marjorie Priceman

How would you make an apple pie if you didn't have what you needed and the grocery store was closed? Why, you'd have to travel around the world to gather the ingredients. You'd find seminola wheat in Italy, milk from a cow in England, and apples in Vermont, and you would make new friends all around the world.

Let's Talk

• Which of these countries would you like to visit. Why?

• What did you learn about baking or where food comes from?

Explore More

• Ask the children to think about one of their favorite foods. Say: *Make a list of all the ingredients you would need to make the food or meal. Think about all the places you would need to go to get the ingredients if you couldn't get them at the store. Cheese isn't really from the store—it comes from cows. Flour isn't really from the store either—it's made from wheat.*

• Throw an apple-tasting party. Without the children seeing you, cut and peel a few varieties of apples and place several slices of each on numbered plates (Gala apples on Plate 1, Braeburn apples on Plate 2, and so on). Give the children an alphabetical list of the types of apples you've sliced, and then have them number their papers. Let them taste each apple and then write down their guess on their paper. See who can correctly guess the most apples.

Focus on Assets
32: Planning and Decision Making
34: Cultural Competence

The Keeping Quilt
by Patricia Polacco

A family who moved from Russia to the United States made a beautiful quilt using material scraps passed down from their Russian relatives to remind them of the homeland they left. Since its creation, the quilt has been passed through four generations of the family—and had been used to wrap babies, make forts, and celebrate weddings—from Russia all the way to the United States.

Let's Talk

- Why was the quilt so important to the Polacco family?

- Does your family have something special that they pass on from older relatives to younger relatives?

Explore More

- Have each child draw a picture of a special family tradition. Place the pictures side by side on a wall to create a quilt.

- Have children use fabric markers to draw a picture of one of their family traditions on a fabric square. Let children present them in a show-and-tell and take them home to keep in a special place.

Focus on Assets
1: Family Support
2: Positive Family Communication

Koala Lou
by Mem Fox
illustrated by Pamela Lofts

Koala Lou misses the love and affection her mother was able to show her before her many siblings came along, and she longs to have some of it back. The solution, she decides, is to win a tree-climbing event in the Bush Olympics, which will demand her mother's attention. Koala Lou does not win the event, but she does realize how much her mother still loves her.

Let's Talk

- Have you ever really wanted to win a game you were playing, but didn't? How did you behave when you lost? How do you hope to behave next time?

- Do you ever question if your parent or guardian *really* loves you? What reminds you that you are loved?

- How do you like family members to show that they love you? How do you show your love to them?

Explore More

- Ask children to draw a tree house and write a story about their family living in the tree house.

- Have children write about why it's important to always give their best regardless of the results.

- Ask: *What do you know about koalas?* Take a trip to the library or look online to find out more about them, such as how they look, what they eat, and where they live.

Focus on Assets
1: Family Support
35: Self-Regulation
38: Self-Esteem

Letting Swift River Go

by Jane Yolen
illustrated by Barbara Cooney

Based on the creation of Quabbin Reservoir, which was made by flooding a valley and several small New England towns, this story is told through the eyes of a 6-year-old girl whose family was forced to move in order for Boston residents to have drinking water. She learns to let go of things from her past and move on.

Let's Talk

• Why did the people have to move?

• How would you feel if you had to move out of your town?

• How do memories help us after we have to let something go?

• Have you ever had to let a person, place, or thing go—like a best friend who moved away, a house or school you had to leave, a puppy who ran away?

• Did things get better after time? How did you let this thing go?

Explore More

• Have children draw a picture of a lake. Then instruct them to turn the page over and draw a picture of what they imagine to be under the lake—not the fish and water, but the roads, trees, and houses that might once have been there.

• Ask the children to think of something that they've had to do that was really sad or hard. Have them write a story or poem about something good that came out of that hard time.

• Make a gelatin lake. Make blue Jell-O according to package directions. Right before you put the Jell-O in the refrigerator to set, add gummy fish into the bowl. The colored fish will be visible beneath the surface of the "water."

Focus on Assets

1: Family Support
4: Caring Neighborhood
27: Equality and Social Justice
40: Positive View of Personal Future

THE EXPERTS WEIGH IN

"It's a reminder that unpleasant changes happen and things may not be the way they were. But you'll always have the memories."

Lana Settle, children's librarian

The Magic Finger

by Roald Dahl

An 8-year-old girl is so upset that her neighbors love to hunt ducks that she uses her magic finger to teach them a lesson—and they will never view life in the same way.

Let's Talk

• What is something that you love and that you think is really important?

• What would you do if you saw someone doing something that you thought was wrong?

• How do you control your temper when you are really angry?

Explore More

• Say: *Hunting made this little girl angry. What is something that makes you angry? It might be something that other people think is normal, or even good.* Then have children write a letter expressing their opinion on this matter and why they think it is an injustice.

• Draw a simple bug outline on a whiteboard and title it "What Bugs Me." Have children share what bugs them and write the ideas inside the bug. Afterward, talk about the items on the whiteboard as a group.

- Say: *Pretend that you have a magic wand that will let you change three things in the world. What will you change? Draw a magic wand on your paper and write a story around the wand and the things you change.*

Focus on Assets

28: Integrity
36: Peaceful Conflict Resolution

Meet Danitra Brown

by Nikki Grimes
illustrated by Floyd Cooper

Zuri Jackson narrates uplifting poems about her best friend, Danitra Brown, praising her ability to deal with insecurities, awkwardness, and social pressure.

Let's Talk

- Which poem did you like the most?

- How do you feel when people make fun of you?

- What are the things you like most about your closest friends?

- How can you be a good friend?

Explore More

- Explore a variety of holidays and have children talk about the different ways people celebrate them.

- Have children create a drawing that revolves around their family culture. Suggest that they include favorite foods, hobbies, rituals, or family members.

- Find a collection of poems from another culture to share with the class. As a group, compare and contrast the focus of these poems with the ones in *Meet Danitra Brown*.

Focus on Assets

33: Interpersonal Competence
34: Cultural Competence
38: Self-Esteem

The Memory Coat

by Elvira Woodruff
illustrated by Michael Dooling

Grisha, an orphan, flees Russia with his cousin Rachel's family. When they reach Ellis Island, a doctor notices a gash near Grisha's eye and marks his coat with chalk to indicate that he is not allowed to enter the United States. Rachel thinks quickly and tells Grisha to turn his coat inside out, hiding the chalk mark.

Let's Talk

- How did Rachel and Grisha support one another when they were bored or afraid?

- What kinds of stories might you and your friends tell through words, pictures, or games?

- Why did Grisha want to keep his old, worn-out coat?

- What do you have that is old and special? Why is it special?

- How would you feel if you had to leave your neighborhood, city, or country?

Explore More

- Have the children imagine that they are stranded on an island. Ask: *What will you do with your free time?* Then have them write a story about their adventures.

- Hold drama time. Invite one child to be the storyteller, who reads *The Memory Coat* while a team of three to five people act it out. Then have the children switch, so different people get a chance to play the various roles.

Mirette on the High Wire
by Emily Arnold McCurly

Mirette meets a daredevil while he is visiting her boardinghouse in Paris. Although she doesn't realize he is the famous tightrope-walking Great Bellini, she admires his ability to walk across the clothesline and asks him to teach her how to do it herself—helping him overcome his own fears in the process.

Let's Talk

• What did the girl learn from the visitor? What did the visitor learn from her?

• What is something you are afraid to do? Why does it make you afraid? What might help you get over your fears?

• What is something you've learned from someone else? What is something you've taught someone else?

Explore More

• Find a few simple magic tricks that you can teach to the children. Talk about learning from other people and books, as well as the courage it takes to share tricks. Then have a special show-and-tell time in which children can demonstrate the magic tricks for other classes or staff.

• Have children design their own circus tent with a high wire. Supply construction paper, tape, straws, paper clips, and pipe cleaners.

• Lay a line of masking tape on the floor for children to use as their own miniature tightrope.

You may also want to check out other books in this series: *Starring Mirette and Bellini* and *Mirette and Bellini Cross Niagara Falls.*

Focus on Assets
8: Children as Resources
16: High Expectations
37: Personal Power

The Mitten
by Jan Brett

When Nicki drops one of his white mittens in the snow, it blends in so well that he can't find it. But the mitten doesn't stay alone for long. Soon several forest animals find it and use it as a cozy place to snuggle up together.

Let's Talk

• What was your favorite part of the story? Why?

• Has anyone ever made anything special for you? What is it and why is it special? How do you take care of it so that it lasts?

• Have you ever made a special gift for someone else? What was it?

Explore More

• Ask children to tell stories to each other about the adventures of their lost sock in the washing machine or the shoe they left in the backyard.

• Have children, with partners, fill magic mittens. Instruct them to trace each of their hands with their fingers held together so that they look like mittens. Then have them cut out the mittens and staple them together along the sides, leaving an opening at the top. Ask each person to write something nice about his partner and put the slip of paper in his mitten. Or, suggest that children give the mitten and a special message to someone special in their life (like the grandma in the story).

Focus on Assets

1: Family Support
2: Positive Family Communication

The Mouse and the Motorcycle

by Beverly Cleary

Ralph the mouse lives alone in a hotel. He longs to see the world beyond his home and gets the chance when he learns to ride a boy's toy motorcycle. He soon finds himself involved in more wild adventures than he had bargained for.

Let's Talk

- What can you learn from Ralph?

- What does this book teach about responsibility?

- What does this book remind you about friendship?

Explore More

- Tell children to imagine that they are a mouse, and one of their favorite toys works like the real thing. Ask children to write a story about their adventure as a mouse with their "real-life" toy.

- Have children decorate their lunch box or a shoe box so it looks like an imaginary vehicle.

- Make edible bikes. Put two sandwich cookies on a piece of paper for the wheels, and then use licorice to make the bike's other parts.

Focus on Assets

1: Family Support
15: Positive Peer Influence
30: Responsibility

Mr. Popper's Penguins

by Richard Atwater
and Florence Atwater

Mr. Popper has a dream—to see the North and South Pole—that he fuels by reading about Admiral Drake and his polar explorations. Mr. Popper writes Admiral Drake a letter of admiration and in return receives a penguin on his doorstep. One penguin quickly becomes a family of twelve, and Mr. Popper hatches the clever idea to take them on the road as entertainers.

Let's Talk

- What do you like about Mr. Popper and his family?

- What is something that makes you as excited as Mr. Popper was about his penguins? What can you do with this excitement?

- Do you have any pets? How can you help take care of your pets?

Explore More

- Ask children to think about their room at home. Then ask: *If penguins came to see your room, what kinds of trouble might they get into?* Then have children draw pictures to show what might happen.

- Visit the library or look online together to see what you can learn about penguins. Have children start a "field journal" and note facts and draw pictures of what they learn.

- Say: *Mr. Popper loved to learn about penguins. What do you like to learn about? Think about all the things you'd like to learn more about, and make a list.* Encourage children to visit the library to check out some books on their favorite new subjects.

- Visit a nursing home or assisted living center and have the children ask elderly residents about their hobbies and passions.

The children can ask questions such as *What do you like to learn about? Why? What are some of the neatest things you've learned?*

Focus on Assets
1: Family Support
26: Caring
33: Interpersonal Competence

Mrs. Piggle-Wiggle

by Betty MacDonald
illustrated by Hilary Knight

All the neighborhood families tap into the wit and wisdom of Mrs. Piggle-Wiggle, who has hysterical remedies for modifying children's behaviors. Children flock to Mrs. Piggle-Wiggle for her crazy, upside-down house, cookies, and treasure-filled backyard. Parents go to her for advice on everything from a child's refusal to bathe to another's painstakingly slow eating.

Let's Talk

• Which character has a hard time doing something that you also have a hard time doing?

• Why is it important to listen and not be rude to parents, teachers, and other adults?

• Why is it important for you to be responsible for your own actions?

Explore More

• Ask: *What good manners do your friends have that even Mrs. Piggle-Wiggle would like?* Have children make a Mrs. Piggle-Wiggle "good manners" award or medal to give to a friend.

• Have children write a story about a fictional child who has really bad manners. Ask: *How does she misbehave? How would Mrs. Piggle-Wiggle help her learn to behave properly?*

Focus on Assets
3: Other Adult Relationships
4: Caring Neighborhood
13: Neighborhood Boundaries
16: High Expectations

My Great-Aunt Arizona

by Gloria Houston
illustrated by Susan Condie Lamb

An Appalachian girl tells the life story of her great-aunt Arizona, who overcame obstacles to become a teacher in the era of the one-room schoolhouse. A teacher for 57 years, she was an inspiration to many throughout her life, especially to her great-niece, who became a teacher herself.

Let's Talk

• How different is your life from the life of the children in the book?

• What would you put in your lunch bucket?

• What is a faraway place that you would like to visit?

• What are things you like to do now that you think you'll still do as you get older?

Explore More

• Ask children to look around your classroom. Ask: *What would be different if you lived when there were only one-room schoolhouses?* Have children draw how the room would be different.

• As a group, look at a map and have children highlight the places they would like to visit. You could also have them mark places where they've already been.

• Say: *In this book, Arizona inspired others to do great things. Who inspires you to try things and to be your best? Write a note thanking this person for setting a good example and inspiring you.*

- Encourage the children to dream. Ask: *What are some of the things you hope to do someday?* Have them make a list to keep in their bedroom or desk, and as they accomplish their goals, they can check them off the list.

Follow-up books for advanced readers are the Little House series by Laura Ingalls Wilder.

Focus on Assets
1: Family Support
14: Adult Role Models
40: Positive View of Personal Future

My Rotten Redheaded Older Brother

by Patricia Polacco

Patricia's older brother, Richard, couldn't be more annoying. He insists on outdoing her in everything, but Patricia is determined to beat him at *something*. After wishing on a falling star, she manages to outlast Richard on a merry-go-round, which renders her so dizzy that she falls. Richard shows his soft side when he scoops up his little sister in his arms and carries her home.

Let's Talk

- Do you have brothers or sisters? Is there someone you love like a brother or sister, such as a cousin or close friend?

- When do you get along best?

- When do you fight?

- What would help you get along better?

Explore More

- Say: *Draw a picture of something you love to do with your brother or sister or best friend. Now draw a picture of something that makes the two of you fight. Turn the picture over, and write one thing you can do to help the two of you get along better or become closer.*

Focus on Assets
1: Family Support
2: Positive Family Communication
33: Interpersonal Competence
36: Peaceful Conflict Resolution

The Paper Bag Princess

by Robert Munsch
illustrated by Michael Martchenko

Elizabeth is a beautiful princess who is engaged to marry the handsome Prince Ronald. A fire-breathing dragon throws their plans off course when he burns all of her fancy clothes and kidnaps her fiancé. Determined to save her prince, Elizabeth dresses in a paper bag and takes off to confront the dragon. When Prince Ronald tells her he doesn't want to be rescued by a princess who looks so awful, she tells him she doesn't want to marry a prince who *is* so awful.

Let's Talk

- How did the princess beat the dragon?

- How did the prince act after the princess saved him? How should he have acted?

- Why is it important to thank people who help us?

- Can you think of a time when you came up with a new way to fix a problem? What was the problem and what did you do to fix it?

Explore More

- Have children finish the following story: *I went to the bathroom to brush my hair. I looked in the mirror, and instead of seeing my own face, I saw a face I'd never seen before! She must have been a princess because she was wearing a crown. She asked me if I was the hero she's been looking for. I said . . .*

- Have children build a castle together out of boxes, canisters, and scrap fabric.

- Ask children to rewrite the story's ending. Ask: *How else might the princess defeat the dragon?*

- Role-play the story using alternate endings.

- Follow another princess in the book *Cinderella*. Then play Cinderella's Shoes on page 133.

Focus on Assets

26: Caring
33: Interpersonal Competence
36: Peaceful Conflict Resolution

Pigsty
by Mark Teague

When Wendell refuses to clean his bedroom, pigs move in and take over, making Wendell's mess even bigger.

Let's Talk

- Why is it important to keep things neat and clean?

- What is one thing that helps you keep your room clean?

- If one of your friends starts to make a mess in your room, what could you do to get this friend to stop?

Explore More

- Have children draw a picture of what their bedroom would look like if they never cleaned it.

- Say: *Imagine that a little creature lives in the middle of your messy room. What does the creature look like? What does he do all day? Write a story about your creature's crazy adventures, and include a picture.*

- Ask children to make a list of reasons it is important to keep their desks and bedrooms cleaned up. Ask: *Why is it hard to keep things clean? What can you do to remind yourself to clean up the next time you make a mess?*

- Have children create a cartoon of themselves cleaning their bedroom or a common living area. Say: *Imagine your parent's reaction. What would your parent say or do if you cleaned this room every week without being asked?*

- Have children finish the following story: *I told my mom I would put my toys in the closet. When I opened the door, I smelled hot chocolate and cotton candy. It seemed to be coming from behind the big, stuffed teddy bear. Before I could move the bear, the closet door closed behind me and . . .*

Focus on Assets

11: Family Boundaries
16: High Expectations
30: Responsibility

Pippi Longstocking
by Astrid Lindgren

Pippi Longstocking is a rambunctious girl who lives alone in her house. Although she has no parents to watch over her, she is kept company by a monkey and a horse. Pippi gets caught up in fanciful adventures every day: one day she'll foil a burglar only to end up dancing with him, and the next she'll play tag with the police.

Let's Talk

- What is something you can do all by yourself?

- What are ways you show responsibility at home? How about at school?

- At home, how do you show that you can be a good leader? What about at school?

Explore More

- Ask: *If Pippi and her friends came to visit you, what would you do together?* Then have children write their own story and draw a picture of themselves with Pippi Longstocking.

- Play Follow the Leader (see page 127), and then talk about the importance of choosing good friends and leaders to follow in real life. Have children write about what happens when they follow good leaders, and what could happen if they follow people who don't make very good choices.

Focus on Assets

11: Family Boundaries
12: School Boundaries
30: Responsibility

The Raft
by Jim LaMarche

Nicky is unhappy that he has to spend the summer with his grandmother instead of with his friends. But things change when he discovers a raft with painted pictures on it that animals are magically drawn to. The raft brings Nicky closer not only to nature and wonder, but to his artist "river rat" grandmother as well.

Let's Talk

- Where did the raft come from? How did Nicky find it?

- Was the boy's summer different than he thought it would be?

- When has something turned out to be different from what you expected?

- Do we sometimes get talents or interests from our grandparents? What talents do you have that your grandmother or grandfather also has? How do you share your talents together?

Explore More

- Have children create rafts out of Popsicle sticks and paint pictures on them.

- Ask the children to form a circle. On a large piece of paper, draw the head of an animal. Pass the paper to the child on the right and ask him to add one body part to the picture. Keep adding parts to your animal until everyone has had a turn. Then instruct children to write or tell a story about this new creature.

Focus on Assets

1: Family Support
2: Positive Family Communication
33: Interpersonal Competence

Rechenka's Eggs
by Patricia Polacco

Babushka is devastated when a wayward goose breaks her beautifully painted, award-winning eggs, but she regains hope when the goose unexpectedly lays exquisitely colored eggs that win Babushka first prize.

Let's Talk

- How did Babushka's bad luck turn into a good thing?

- How do you respond when you have bad luck?

- How do you respond when you have good luck?

Explore More

- Have children write an alternative ending to *Rechenka's Eggs*.

- Have children write a story about something bad in their life that turned into something good.

- Have children draw and color their own exquisite egg.

- Visit a library with the children and borrow a book on egg decoration, and then have children try some of the ideas.

Focus on Assets
37: Personal Power
39: Sense of Purpose
40: Positive View of Personal Future

The Relatives Came

by Cynthia Rylant
illustrated by Stephen Gammell

Relatives pile into a car and travel to visit family between grape-picking seasons. The funny illustrations help tell the story of the memories they make together.

Let's Talk
- What memories did the family make together?

- How did they make room for all of the people?

- Do friends or family members ever stay at your home? What do you do together? Where do people sleep?

Explore More
- Use this writing prompt. Ask: *How do your family members let you know they care about you? How do they show you that they love you?*

- Have children draw pictures to illustrate what they like to do when relatives or family friends come to visit.

Focus on Assets
1: Family Support
2: Positive Family Communication

Roxaboxen

by Alice McLerran
illustrated by Barbara Cooney

The residents of Roxaboxen are all children, and the only rule is that rules are made up as you go along. In this make-believe town situated in a desert of rocks, the mayor is a child, and the citizens are bound only by their imaginations.

Let's Talk
- What do you like to do in your free time?

- If there were no electricity, what games would you play with your friends? How would you spend your time?

- Have you ever played a game using things you found around you, like rocks, paper, sticks, or boxes? What did you use and what did you play?

Explore More
- Create a game. Divide children into two groups. Place before them a sample of supplies, including objects such as straws,

THE EXPERTS WEIGH IN

"If you're not familiar with Alice McLerran's *Roxaboxen*, you've got to read it soon! It's about how children used to play, making up games with the neighborhood kids and playing outside all day long. It really is lovely, and it makes me worry a bit for children today; they don't get much organic problem-solving experience anymore."

Susan Poulter, children's librarian

paper plates and cups, and plastic forks and spoons. Give each group a piece of paper and have them select two items from those offered. Allow each group 15 minutes to create a game, name it, and design a television commercial to advertise it using the supplies they've chosen.

- Create an obstacle course outdoors for the children to race through.

- Make nature sculptures. Gather natural materials, such as tree bark, rocks, grass, leaves, and so on. Have children make a base with the tree bark or a rock and decorate it with the other natural objects you've gathered.

Focus on Assets

17: Creative Activities
37: Personal Power
40: Positive View of Personal Future

Sadako and the Thousand Paper Cranes

by Eleanor Coerr
illustrated by Ronald Himler

After Sadako is diagnosed and hospitalized with an illness caused by an atom bomb, she begins making origami cranes to keep herself busy, with the goal of completing 1,000. She dies before achieving that goal, however, at 644 cranes. Her classmates finish the remaining cranes, and Sadako is buried with all 1,000.

Let's Talk

- What does it mean to have hope?

- What is a symbol of hope for you?

- What do you do when you're really sad?

- How do you help other people when they are sad or afraid?

Explore More

- Take children to the library to learn more about Hiroshima.

- Have children create their own symbol of hope through art. Supply play dough, papier-mâché, paper, paint, and markers.

- Ask children to write about a time when they were really sad and to include what gave them hope.

- Make paper cranes and let the group give them to someone who is sick.

Focus on Assets

26: Caring
33: Interpersonal Competence
34: Cultural Competence

Saturdays and Teacakes

by Lester L. Laminack
illustrated by Chris Soentpiet

Every Saturday, a little boy rides his bike to visit his grandmother. They spend the day together, working in the yard, listening to blue jays, and eating homemade teacakes.

Let's Talk

- How did the boy stay safe while he was on his bicycle?

- How did the boy help his grandmother?

- What special memories did the boy and his grandmother make together?

- Do you have grandparents? What are some special things you can do together to make memories?

Explore More

- Ask children to write down a few ways they can help one of their grandparents or another older adult.

- Invite someone to talk to the group about bicycle or scooter safety. Then encourage the children to teach a younger child how to ride safely.

- Have children draw a picture of one of their favorite memories or activities with a grandparent or other special adult.

Focus on Assets
1: Family Support
3: Other Adult Relationships
10: Safety
14: Adult Role Models

The Spyglass: A Book about Faith
by Richard Paul Evans
illustrated by Jonathan Linton

A little village falls into poverty and loses hope until a stranger visits the town with a spyglass that magically transforms the community.

Let's Talk

- How did the spyglass help the kingdom?

- How did hope change the people and the king in this story?

- What gives you hope when bad things happen?

- What would you like to change about your life at home, at school, or in your neighborhood?

- How can you start making these changes today?

Explore More

- Encourage further discussion. Say: *Pretend you have a magic spyglass that can see the future of your family, your school, or your neighborhood. What do you see? What can you do to help make sure there is a happy future?*

- Have children make a spyglass using a cardboard paper towel holder, then let them walk around and look at their world

through it. Ask them to make a list of things they would like to change and to ask a parent or another caring adult to help them start working toward that change.

Focus on Assets
37: Personal Power
40: Positive View of Personal Future

Stella Louella's Runaway Book
by Lisa Campbell Ernst

When a little girl loses her library book, she discovers in her search that everyone, from the mailperson to the police officer to the woman at the diner, has also enjoyed reading her book.

Let's Talk

- What do you think the book was about?

- What is the librarian's favorite part of the book? Why?

- What is one of your favorite books? Do you know someone else who likes your favorite book? Who is it?

- Have you ever lost something that was important to you? What was it?

Explore More

- Invite children to make up a story about losing something. Ask: *Where does your lost item go? Who enjoys it while it's gone? How do you finally find it?*

- Have each child pick out a book and then put a note on the inside cover, inviting other readers to please enjoy reading the book, write their name on the list, and share the book with another friend. Then have children give the book to someone else, and set a due date to see how many people get a chance to read it before the time is up. You can limit this activity to your own group or expand it.

- Have children make their own books by folding several sheets of paper together down the middle and stapling them. If you have enough time, you can allow them to put in a little more effort. Let aspiring artists paint their paper whatever color they want before putting the book together. Let the paper dry overnight. Then cut the sheets into a standard size (for example, 5 x 7 or 8 x 10) and bind them either by stapling them together on the left side or by punching holes on the left side and connecting them with plastic rings or yarn. Transform a paperback into a hardcover by folding cardstock paper or cardboard over the outside of the book.

Focus on Assets
4: Caring Neighborhood
25: Reading for Pleasure

The Stories Julian Tells

by Ann Cameron
illustrated by Ann Strugnell

Julian loves to make up outrageous stories to tell his family and friends. He especially likes to trick his little brother, Huey, into believing everything he says. The mischief will have you laughing out loud.

Let's Talk

- Which of Julian's stories was your favorite? Why?

- What's the most important lesson Julian learned?

- What did this book teach you about being a good friend?

Explore More

- Ask children to write a funny story about their family.

- Have children write their own story about something silly that might happen in Julian's family.

- Ask children to think about a time they did something that wasn't nice. Tell them to write what happened but to give the story a different ending, in which they made better choices. Have them discuss whether the true account or the fictional story had a happier ending and why.

- Find a long word in the dictionary and read it aloud to the children. Have them make up their own definition, write it on a piece of paper, and pass the paper to you. Have the real definition written on your own piece of paper. Then mix the papers and read the definitions aloud. See if the children can guess which definition is correct. Encourage them to try to remember the real definition.

Focus on Assets
1: Family Support
33: Interpersonal Competence

Thunder Cake

by Patricia Polacco

A little girl is terribly afraid of storms. But she finds relief through her grandmother, who distracts her by baking a cake while the storm is coming.

Let's Talk

- Why was the little girl afraid?

- How did she get over her fears?

- What scares you?

- What can you do to overcome your fears?

Explore More

- Have children write a different ending to the story. Ask: *If she hadn't gotten over her fears, what would have happened?*

- Say: *Your fairy godmother has offered to take away one of your biggest fears. What fear will she take away? Draw a picture of your fairy godmother helping you to be brave.*

- Ask children to write down all the things they imagine rolling around in the sky to cause thunder. Have them draw a picture of one of the things they imagine. Then, as a class, research the real cause of thunder.

- Have the children write a poem about the many different kinds of weather.

Focus on Assets
1: Family Support
3: Other Adult Relationships

Toys Go Out: Being the Adventures of a Knowledgeable Stingray, a Toughy Little Buffalo, and Someone Called Plastic

by Emily Jenkins
illustrated by Paul O. Zelinsky

Little Girl's best friends are StingRay, Lumphy, and Plastic, toys that come alive and experience daring adventures, all told through a series of beautiful black-and-white illustrations.

Let's Talk

- What was your favorite story in the book and why?

- Who was your favorite character and why?

- Do you have a toy that you like to pretend is alive? If you could talk with the toy, what would you talk about? What do you pretend is your toy's favorite thing to do?

Pair together with *The Velveteen Rabbit* as a companion book. See page 108.

Explore More

- Have children pick one of the characters in the book and then act out another adventure it might take.

- Play partner games such as a three-legged race. After you play, talk about the importance of friendship and how to build and maintain healthy friendships.

- Watch the movie *Toy Story*, then talk about similarities and differences between the story lines in this book and the movie.

- Have the children write about one of their favorite book or television characters. Ask: *Who is this favorite character? What if this character became real in your life? What would you talk about or do together? What would you like to know about the character?*

Focus on Assets
2: Positive Family Communication
32: Planning and Decision Making
37: Personal Power

Train to Somewhere

by Eve Bunting
illustrated by Ronald Himler

Marianne rides the "Orphan Train" from a New York City orphanage to reunite with her mother, who has gone west to prepare a new life for her daughter. When Marianne arrives, though, her mother is nowhere to be found, and she is instead adopted by a kind elderly couple who teach her that sometimes when life goes off track it can be for the best.

Let's Talk

- How do you think Marianne felt when

more and more of her friends were being adopted by families at the station?

- How do you think she felt as she waited for her mother?

- How do you think she felt when she first met her new adoptive mother?

- What gives you hope when life is difficult?

- Share a time when something sad that happened in your life had a happy ending.

Explore More

- Ask children to write a poem about their family. Say: *Within the poem, list all the things you're thankful for about your family.*

THE EXPERTS WEIGH IN

Lana Settle, a children's librarian, uses these two writing assignments with her students:

Say: *Imagine you were a member of a family waiting to adopt a child from the Orphan Train. Write a story telling how you will welcome this new child into your family and help her feel loved.*

Say: *Write a journal entry about your own experiences as an orphan. You may choose one of the following ideas to help you get started: I am an Orphan Train rider; I am an orphan on the streets of New York City; or I am a member of the Orphan Train rider's new family.*

- Say: *Pay attention to those around you who don't have family support. Look for opportunities to invite them to do things with your family.* Then have children discuss the kind of situations they might encounter.

Focus on Assets
1: Family Support

The True Story of the Three Little Pigs
by Jon Scieszka
illustrated by Lane Smith

Alexander T. Wolf insists that he's just misunderstood—he never meant to hurt those pigs! He needed a cup of sugar for the cake he was baking for his grandma, and he had to go door-to-door, hoping for neighbors who would share some. His awful cold made him sneeze and knock down all the walls. The whole thing was an accident.

Let's Talk

- How do you know when someone is telling the truth?

- Can there be two sides to the truth, even when they are very different? Why or why not?

- Why is it important to tell the truth?

Explore More

- Have children think of their favorite fairy tales. Ask them to pick one and think of a new ending. Have children share their new endings with the group.

- Lay out a specific scenario by saying: *Imagine that your aunt makes a sweater for you and gives it to you as a gift. However, you don't like the sweater. You love your aunt, so you don't want to hurt her feelings. What would you do or say to thank her for her kindness without saying you love the sweater?* Discuss the children's answers.

- Play Two Truths and a Lie. Ask the children to think about two truths and one lie about themselves. Taking turns, have each child share his three statements without revealing which one is false. The other children should try to guess which statement is untrue. Then talk about the importance of honesty.

- Play the Story Perspectives game on page 123.

If you want to continue exploring fairy tales, read "Jack and the Beanstalk," and try these related activities: Ask children to use pinto beans to create simple shapes, and then let others guess the magic picture. Or ask children to write their own fairy tale ending. Give them this prompt: *When Jack went to buy the magic beans, the guy was all out, so instead he bought . . .*

Focus on Assets
29: Honesty

The Velveteen Rabbit

by Margery Williams

This classic tale demonstrates how a child's love can bring a stuffed animal to life.

Let's Talk

- How did the other toys treat the Rabbit when he first came to the nursery?

- How did the Skin Horse make the Rabbit feel better?

- How do you know the boy loved the Rabbit?

- How can you be a good friend using your words and actions?

Explore More

- Have children write a story about their favorite stuffed animal or toy. Ask: *Who are her friends? What are her favorite things to do? Where does she like to go? What makes her happiest?*

- Invite children to bring their favorite stuffed animal in for show-and-tell.

- Have children finish the following story: *I was taking a nice nap with my favorite stuffed animal. When I woke up, I rubbed my eyes, looked around, and saw that I wasn't at home anymore! I was in the middle of a field. I stood up and . . .*

- Hold a Bunny Hop Relay. Divide the group into relay teams. Have the first child on each team place a potato between his knees and hop to the finish line and back. The child should then tag the next person in line, who puts the potato between his knees and does the same. The first team to finish wins the race.

Focus on Assets
26: Caring
33: Interpersonal Competence

Weslandia

by Paul Fleischman
illustrated by Kevin Hawkes

A bullied little boy who feels left out channels his frustration into amazingly creative dreams and develops his own city. In time, everyone wants to be involved, and so the formerly left-out child ends the book with plenty of friends.

Let's Talk

- What does it mean to be frustrated? What helped the boy get past his frustration to do something good and positive for himself?

- What did the boy do to turn things around?

- When things aren't going so well, how can you turn things around? What power do you have to make things better? How can your attitude, words, or actions affect or change things?

- What would you have done if you were the boy? How would you have responded to his situation?

- What would you have created?

Explore More

- Have children bring a box of items they enjoy using when they're on their own (e.g., stickers, puzzles, crayons, coloring books). When children finish homework early or have free time, let them choose an activity from their box.

- Have children imagine a new invention. Ask them to draw a picture of it and write about what it does.

- Say: *What are fun things you can do to keep you out of trouble? Work with a partner to see how many fun things you can think of to do alone or with a friend.*

- Using a lemon and premade lemonade, teach children how something good can come out of something bad. Have children taste a drop of lemon juice, and then give them a taste of lemonade to compare it with. Ask: *What did it take for something sour to become something sweet? How can you turn sour situations into something sweet?* Discuss their answers. Then have them write positive messages on burlap that they can put up at home to help them remember that they have the power to turn things around through their attitudes and actions.

Focus on Assets

37: Personal Power
38: Self-Esteem
39: Sense of Purpose

When Jessie Came across the Sea

by Amy Hest
illustrated by P. J. Lynch

Little Jessie travels away from her precious grandmother in Eastern Europe to the United States, where she sews lace for a dressmaker. Eventually, she is able to save enough money for a ticket so her grandmother can come and join her.

Let's Talk

- Was it hard for Jessie's grandmother to let her go to the United States? Why was she willing to let her go? Are good decisions always easy?

- How did Jessie and her grandmother continue to show their love for each other even though they were far apart?

- Why did Jessie ask her grandmother to keep her mother's wedding ring?

- Why is it so important to learn to read and write?

Explore More

- Have children make their own paper doll boy or girl. Give them paper and scissors to cut one out, and then have them design a hat or an outfit for their paper doll to wear.

- Help children find a pen pal in another country. Tell them they can write letters to one another and see what each can learn from the other.

Focus on Assets

1: Family Support
2: Positive Family Communication
34: Cultural Competence

The Wonderful Happens

by Cynthia Rylant
illustrated by Coco Dowley

In this book, the author uses cause and effect to explain everyday wonders—that bread comes from flour, birds come from eggs, roses come from seeds—and to tell children they are special and that they came from somewhere, too.

Let's Talk

- What does it mean to be grateful?

- What are you grateful for today?

- What would the world be missing if you weren't in it?

Explore More

- Take the children on a nature walk. Have them bring their journals so they can look around and write down all the wonderful things they see, hear, and feel. When you return, ask the children to write a poem about the wonderful things they experienced around them.

- Put birdseed in a feeder outside. Have children take note of the different varieties of birds that visit the feeders. After a few weeks, ask: *How many kinds did you see? How are they different from each other?*

Focus on Assets

37: Personal Power
38: Self-Esteem
40: Positive View of Personal Future

Yoko

by Rosemary Wells

When Yoko's classmates laugh at the sushi in her lunch box, her teacher announces an International Food Day, during which everyone will try all different kinds of foods. Yoko and Timothy discover a love for multicultural food and decide to open their own restaurant.

Let's Talk

- What foods from other countries have you tried?

- What new foods would you like to try?

- If you could open a restaurant, what kind of food would you serve?

Explore More

- Bring fortune cookies for each child. After the children enjoy their cookies and fortunes, have them write a new fortune that wishes others well.

- Invite someone from Japan or someone who has been to Japan to have tea with the class. Ask him to share information about the tea ceremony and its importance in Japanese culture.

- Eat lunch outside and enjoy new finger foods together.

- Host a blindfold taste test to see if children can guess what different foods are without being able to see them.

- Say: *A lunch box with your name on it mysteriously appears. The card attached to it says you should open it if you are brave and hungry. You open it and find . . .* Have children share their responses.

- Expand children's sensory experiences by playing the Guessing Game on page 134.

Focus on Assets

34: Cultural Competence

Play and Move

Discovery takes place through the world of play. Play allows us to tap into our potential—to take the promise within and bring it forth to make a difference without. When we help children foster their own sense of capacity (abilities, talents, empathy, understanding, and compassion) as well as curiosity and creativity, we can help them become healthier individuals, more well rounded and whole.

The games included in this unit are categorized by themes intended to do just that. They range from Community-Building Games and a focus on relationships and getting-to-know-you activities to Follow the Leader Games for establishing norms, and a variety of team-building games that build an array of skills through a broad range of activities meant to appeal to the various types of learners in your group. There are also Backward Play Games that call upon a depth of trust, and, last but certainly not least, games that challenge your team to solve problems (Puzzles, Marathon Events, and Scavenger Hunts).

Each game can be tied to several assets, which are listed at the end. As in previous units, each item is followed by a section called Let's Talk that includes questions and opportunities for sharing, which you can use to take the game just that much further—to apply life lessons and connect the dots to character and assets. So, get moving and get active! Do a puzzle. Do a scavenger hunt. Play Follow the Leader. Or host your own Olympic event. Whatever game you choose, let the children have fun and play hard. Plato said, "You can learn more about a person from an hour of play than from a year of conversation." That hour is well spent building inner strength and character while letting children simply be who they are.

Human Bingo

Time: 5 minutes

You Will Need: A bingo card and pencil for each person

Preparation: Make a 4 x 4 grid (bingo card) of accomplishments or skills that children in your group might have. You might include things like "plays an instrument," "speaks another language," or "competes in a sport."

Distribute a bingo card and pencil to each player. Instruct children to mingle around the room to find players who have the skills or accomplishments listed in the boxes and ask these players to write their name in the box that pertains to them. Players can sign each card only one time, and they can sign a box only if it describes something they have done. The first three or four people who fill all the boxes with unique signatures and call "Bingo" win the game.

Let's Talk

• What new things did you learn about each other?

• What did you learn about yourself?

• How did it feel when you could sign a square on someone's card?

• Why is it important to notice other people's skills and talents?

Focus on Assets
33: Interpersonal Competence
38: Self-Esteem
39: Sense of Purpose

Hot Potato Toss

Time: 5–10 minutes

You Will Need: A small beanbag, music, a list of questions or prompts related to positive values, such as the following:

• Who is someone you look up to because that person does good things?

• How do you show people you care about them?

• How do you show respect for people who are different from you?

• Talk about a time you told the truth, even when it was hard to do.

Have the children sit in a circle, and then play the music. Have them pass the beanbag clockwise around the circle. When you stop the music, the person holding the beanbag must answer out loud one of the questions you've prepared. After she answers the question, start the music again and keep playing until all the questions have been answered by someone.

Let's Talk

• Why is it important to have strong values?

• Why is it important to talk with others about our values?

• What happens if we don't stay true to our values?

Focus on Assets
26: Caring
28: Integrity
29: Honesty

I Know You, Friend!

Time: 5–10 minutes

You Will Need: One chair

Tell the group that they're going to play a game to see how well they know each other and how well they can recognize each other's voices. Select one player to be "it" and to sit in a chair with his back to the rest of the group. Have another player approach and say, "I know you, [name of person who is "it"]." The person approaching can speak in her normal voice or disguise it. The person sitting should then say, "I know you, friend. You're [name of person he thinks it is]." If he has guessed correctly, then the other player becomes the new guesser. If he has guessed incorrectly, then he can guess one more time. If he still guesses incorrectly, then a new player should approach the person for him to guess. Let the guesser continue until he identifies someone correctly or three turns have been completed, whichever happens first.

Let's Talk

• How does it feel to enter a room in which people know you?

• How does it feel to be called by name?

• How did it feel when the person didn't know you right away?

• What are some things you'd like other people to know about you? Why is that important to you?

• What can you do to help you remember other people's names?

Focus on Assets
5: Caring School Climate
33: Interpersonal Competence
38: Self-Esteem

Smile

Time: 5–10 minutes

Have the children gather in a circle. Choose one player to be Smiley, whose goal is to get someone in the circle to smile; the rest of the circle group should try their best not to smile. Smiley can tell jokes and make funny faces, gestures, or sounds, but cannot touch the people in the circle. If Smiley makes someone smile, he should hug that person, who will join the original Smiley in the next round of play. Now they will both try to make people smile. Continue the game and count how many people are smiling by the end of a set time limit (three to four minutes).

Let's Talk

• How easy was it to make others smile?

• Who in your life makes you smile?

• Do you make other people smile? Who are they? What do you do to make them smile?

• How can a smile or laugh make your day?

• In this game, the Smileys brought both smiles and hugs. What can you do every day to help make other people happy?

Focus on Assets
26: Caring
33: Interpersonal Competence
39: Sense of Purpose

I Like People Who Like . . .

Time: 5–15 minutes

You Will Need: Chairs (one fewer than the number of people playing)

Put the chairs in a circle. Have everyone sit, with one player standing in the middle of the group. That player will start the game by saying her name, something she likes about herself, and filling in the statement "I like people who like . . ." (For example, children might say: pizza, football, swimming, vanilla ice cream.) Everyone who likes that very same thing should get up and, along with the person who made the statement, find a different seat in the circle (one that is not right beside their current seat). The person left without a seat will say his name, something he likes about himself, and "I like people who like . . ." Repeat as often as desired. The goal is to get everyone in the middle at least once.

Let's Talk

After asking the following questions, have the group make cards for the people they care about. They can describe the game they played and share what it is they like about each card recipient.

- Who is someone you care about? What do you like about this person?

- How can we show others that we like them?

- How can we tell the people we care about what we like about them?

Focus on Assets

5: Caring School Climate
26: Caring
33: Interpersonal Competence
38: Self-Esteem

My Friend

Time: 5–10 minutes

Break the group into pairs. Have one person interview the other person for one minute. When the minute is up, have each person sit back-to-back with her partner. Choose one pair to start, and ask the interviewer to answer the following without looking at her partner:

- What color eyes does your partner have?

- What color is your partner's shirt?

- What kind of shoes is your partner wearing?

- Is your partner wearing a belt? Eyeglasses?

- Is your partner missing his front teeth?

Repeat with as many pairs as you wish.

Variation: Have friends volunteer to pair up. Have them sit back-to-back, and ask them a series of questions in which one friend will predict what the other will say. You might ask a series of "favorite" questions, such as the other person's favorite book, flavor of ice cream, pet, sport, school subject. After asking each question, give the pair time to think, with one of the players drawing or writing his answers on paper. Then have them face each other to give their answers. The vocal friend should answer first while the other remains silent. Then the silent partner should reveal his written or drawn answer to see if the partners' answers match.

Let's Talk

- This game was sneaky. You had to pay attention. How can you really pay attention to others when you spend time with them?

- What can you do to find the good things about other people?

- Why is it important to spend time with friends and show them you really care about them?

Focus on Assets

15: Positive Peer Influence
33: Interpersonal Competence
34: Cultural Competence

Spinning a Yarn

Time: 10–15 minutes

You Will Need: A ball of yarn

Use this activity when you're reviewing homework or a subject the group is exploring. Have the children gather in a circle. Then have one player hold the end of the yarn and toss the ball of it to another player. The person who tosses the ball of yarn should ask the person who catches it a homework-related question. The player who catches it should answer the question, hold on to her place at that length of the yarn, and then toss the ball to someone else, asking that person a new question. Keep the game going until everyone has had a turn both asking and answering a question. Then reverse the process to wind the ball of yarn back into its original shape.

Note: With the reversal, you can also reverse the review process. Have a person give an answer that the next player must come up with a question for.

Variation 1–Telling a Story:
The first person should give the first line of a story and pass the yarn. The next player should continue the story with her own line and twist. As the yarn continues along, so does the story. Challenge players to have their story reach a climax by the time it gets to the last person, and then as the yarn is reversed and wound back up, they can problem-solve to bring the story to a solution or conclusion.

Variation 2–At a Party:
Create some general questions or questions based on a specific theme for children to answer as they toss the yarn to one another. Themes might include favorite books, favorite board games, or favorite sports.

Let's Talk

• What was your favorite part of the game?

• What's one thing you'll remember from today?

• Why do you think you'll be able to remember it?

Focus on Assets
21: Achievement Motivation
24: Bonding to School
32: Planning and Decision Making

Cub Reporter

Time: 5–10 minutes

You Will Need: Paper and pencils (optional)

Tell the group that they are part of the *Daily Grind* newspaper and television news program and that today's assignment is to find interesting people, or most valuable persons (MVPs) to spotlight in the paper and on the show. Have the group come up with five or six questions to ask their subjects. Children could ask about favorite colors, foods, or hobbies.

Break the group into pairs. Designate one person to be the cub reporter from the *Daily Grind* and the other the MVP. Give time for the cub reporters to ask three interview questions, and then let them take turns introducing their MVP to the whole group. Each reporter can decide how she wants to introduce her MVP, what facts she wants to share about this person, and what she likes best about her MVP.

Variation: For advanced readers, and to help emphasize reading, distribute a list of 10 interview questions and direct reporters to select 3 from the list.

Let's Talk

• What new things did you learn about the person you interviewed?

• Did you find out that you have things in common with this person?

- Was it hard to answer questions about yourself? If so, why?

- Was there a question you wanted the other person to ask you? What was the question?

- Why is that question important to you?

Focus on Assets
32: Planning and Decision Making
33: Interpersonal Competence
34: Cultural Competence

What Makes Me "Me"

Time: 5 minutes

Call out various characteristics people have (avoiding physical traits). Say, *Stand if this fits you*, and then fill in the rest of the sentence with a characteristic, such as: *I like to color. I have a younger brother. I am the oldest. I like pizza. I think it's fun to play sports. I like to read.* If the given characteristic fits, players should stand up. Give the players a moment to see who else is standing, and then ask them to sit down again before you call out the next trait.

Let's Talk

- Were you in a group at least once with every other player? (If many players say yes, point out that we all have *something* in common with everyone else. If many players say no, say that if you had continued the game you would have found something in common with everyone.)

- Why is it important to find things you have in common with others?

Focus on Assets
5: Caring School Climate
33: Interpersonal Competence
34: Cultural Competence

Gossip or Telephone

Time: 5–10 minutes

You Will Need: A small piece of paper and a pen

Have everyone sit in a circle. Write down a two- to four-sentence statement, and then whisper it into the first player's ear. Tell that person to whisper it into the next person's ear, and so on, until the original statement goes all the way around the group to the last person. Ask that player to say what she heard, and compare her statement to the statement you wrote on the piece of paper.

Let's Talk

- How close was the last statement to the statement written on the piece of paper?

- What could have helped the statement stay the same until the last player heard it?

- Have you ever heard something and then found out you heard it wrong? Did it make a difference or did anything happen because you didn't hear it correctly?

- Do you ever have trouble hearing what someone is saying? If you don't understand what someone has said, do you ask the person to repeat it?

- Sometimes the wrong information gets spread to other people. Has anyone ever told other people something about you that was wrong?

Focus on Assets
5: Caring School Climate
15: Positive Peer Influence
26: Caring
28: Integrity

Give Me an A! B! C!

Time: 5–10 minutes

Invite players to come up with as many words as they can to describe their classroom (or home, school, or neighborhood). The only rules are that (1) the words must be descriptive, (2) they must be positive, (3) they must all start with the same letter, and (4) they cannot be repeated.

Start at one end of the group. The first person might say, "My class is an *awesome* class." Then the next person might say something like, "My class is an *active* class." Continue on until everyone has described the class using the letter *A*.

If someone repeats a word or cannot think of a new word within a count of five, he can redeem himself and start with the next letter of the alphabet to describe the location (e.g., "My class is a *brave* class"), but he has one strike against him. A player is out if he repeats a word or gets three strikes in a row. Keep track of the number of adjectives the group comes up with.

Want to make it even more fun? Create a beat that the group can keep going—similar to the beat in the old game The Minister's Cat. That game is based on a 10-beat vocal rhythm in which children supply one two-beat word (*cra-zy*) to describe the cat each time the phrase is said. If a participant can't think of a word to say on the two beats, then she's out. The next person restarts the game using the next letter of the alphabet.

Let's Talk

• Words are powerful. How can you remember to say more nice things about others rather than mean things?

• What should you do if someone says something mean to you? How can you respond in a nice way?

• How do you feel when someone says something nice about you?

Focus on Assets
5: Caring School Climate
26: Caring
33: Interpersonal Competence

Spelling Beat

Time: 5–10 minutes

Play as one big group or break into small groups. Have the players stand in a circle. Name a word for the participants to spell. Explain that they will spell out the word, with each player saying one letter of the word as they take turns clockwise around the circle. But here's where the activity gets tricky. Tell the children that for every *consonant* they say aloud, they must at the same time hop on *two feet*. For every *vowel* spoken, the speller must at the same time hop on *one foot*. Encourage them to listen to the rhythms the words form.

Let's Talk

• How did it feel to have to say the letter out loud and move at the same time? Was it fun or did it feel too hard to do? Why?

• How do you handle it when things in life get hard?

Focus on Assets
22: School Engagement
31: Healthy Lifestyle

ABC Stack-Up

Time: 5 minutes

You Will Need: Alphabet cards and wild cards. You can make your own by writing one letter of the alphabet on each of 26–52 blank cards (26 for one full set of alphabet letters, 52 for two full sets). Just make sure there are enough for each student to have one card. Include a few wild cards in the mix by drawing a symbol of some sort on several of the blank cards. (The number of wild cards you'll need depends on the size of your group. If your group has 10 or fewer participants, one or two wild cards will suffice. If your group has more than 50 participants, you'll need five or six wild cards.)

Distribute one card to each player, making sure that several get a wild card. Give the players 30 seconds or less to mingle and come up with as many two-letter words (*go, to, by*) as they can, reminding them that a wild card can be used as any letter. When time is called, note how many words were made, how many people were able to create two-letter words, and what letters were left out during the round.

In the second round, within the same amount of time, have the group come up with three-letter words (*get, big, red*). Note how many words were made, how many people were involved, and what letters were left out.

In the third round, have the group attempt to spell out four-letter words (*high, tree, team*). Note how many words were made, how many people were involved, and what letters were left out.

Let's Talk

• What words were the easiest to make? Two-letter, three-letter, or four-letter words?

• Raise your hand if you were left out of forming a word one time. Two times? Three times?

• In which round, one, two, or three, did you have to think the hardest?

• In which round did you need to work with other people the most?

• Why is it important to learn to work well with other people?

Focus on Assets

5: Caring School Climate
21: Achievement Motivation
32: Planning and Decision Making

What's in a Word?

Time: 3–10 minutes

You Will Need: Paper, pencils

Break the group into smaller teams of three to six players. Give the group a compound word or phrase (*firefighter* or *happy birthday*) and have teams come up with as many words as possible using the letters from the word or phrase only as many times as they originally appear. Give them a time limit of one minute. Keep tabs on the number of words created by each team.

For a bigger challenge, play several rounds, giving a new word or phrase for each one and decreasing the time in which to form words. (Round One: 1 minute, Round Two: 45 seconds, Round Three: 30 seconds, Round Four, or "Speed Round": 15 seconds.)

Recognize various talents, such as Speedy Spellers—those with the highest word total from all rounds—teams with the Biggest Word of the Day, the Most Interesting Word of the Day, the Hardest Word of the Day, Best Noun, Best Adjective, Best Verb, and Favorite Word of the Day (let the players vote on this one).

Let's Talk

• When you first looked at the big word, all you saw was that one word. But when you looked closer, you were able to find other words. Is there something you want to learn that seems really big?

• How can you break that big thing into small steps?

• How is it easier when you work hard on something with a friend?

Rhymes Scramble

Time: 5 minutes

You Will Need: Pre-made index cards that feature portions of a nursery rhyme

Write each phrase of a favorite nursery rhyme on its own index card. Distribute one to each player.

Sample division:

• Hickory, dickory, dock

• The mouse ran up the clock

Have players mingle, reading each card and attempting to put the phrases in the correct order. When they are done, read the rhyme out loud, checking for accuracy against the full nursery rhyme. If you are working with an advanced group, have them compete against the clock to see how fast they can put their rhyme in the proper order.

Variation: Write portions of math equations on cards and distribute them. Have players mingle to find the correct match. Example: Card A shows *2 + 2*; Card A's match shows *= 4.* Or use sentence portions to allow students more random, creative expression. Example: Card A reads *the flower*, Card B reads *blooms in spring*, Card C reads *the cat*, Card D reads *is sleeping*, and so on. Have players mingle to create their own sentences. Allow them to be creative in how they match the cards. The cat could be sleeping, *or* the flower could be sleeping.

Let's Talk

• This game is like a recipe with ingredients,

like for a cake. What are the ingredients for caring? How do you show others you care about them?

• You had to make decisions in this game—you had to decide which cards went with other cards. How do you make good decisions in real life, at school and at home?

Explore More

For more rhyming fun, see the activities with David McPhail's book *Those Can-Do Pigs* on page 79.

Focus on Assets
5: Caring School Climate
32: Planning and Decision Making
37: Personal Power

The Changing Word Game

Time: 5–10 minutes

Sit in a circle with the players. Say "A." Turn to the player next to you and tell her to think of a word that starts with *A* but to *say* only the next letter (example: "P"). The next player should add the third letter, or, if he can't think of a word that starts with *A* and *P*, he can challenge the second person and say, "I don't think she has a word to spell!" The challenged player should respond by saying the word she was thinking of—*apple*. In this case the challenger was wrong and gets a strike. If the challenger *is* correct (for example, if the second person says *appe* instead of *ape*), then the second person would get a strike.

For older children, add in another chance to get a strike if a player gets stuck with the last letter of the word. Challenge players to keep thinking ahead so that they're prepared to make the word change as it gets closer to being spelled out. For example, a player about to come to the *Y* in *pony* could offer the letter *I* instead, changing the word to *ponies* and thus avoiding a strike.

- In this game, did you ever think the letters were going to make up a certain word, but the person was thinking of a different word instead?

- Have you ever thought you knew what someone was going to say and interrupted him instead of letting him finish talking?

- Is it ever good manners to interrupt someone? What should we do instead?

- When you make a bad choice, what can you do to make things better?

- What should you do if you have a friend who gets you in trouble?

Focus on Assets

28: Integrity
29: Honesty
33: Interpersonal Competence
37: Personal Power

Alphabet Soup

Time: 5–15 minutes

You Will Need: Three index cards per person, pens, one piece of paper per team of four to six players

Give three index cards to each person. Ask the players to write down a different letter of the alphabet on each card, without showing their cards to anyone else. They can choose any letters they wish as long as they don't repeat letters.

Break the large group into smaller teams of four to six players. Distribute one piece of paper to each team. Give the teams four minutes to create as many words as possible out of the letters they have in their group. When time is up, see what words were created and how many each team came up with. Play several rounds, combining or mixing up teams. Award points for shortest word, longest word, most words, most creative word, and so on.

Let's Talk

- How did you decide which letters you would use?

- How did you and your teammates work together to create each new word?

- How did you work with your teammates to solve any trouble you were having forming new words?

Focus on Assets

32: Planning and Decision Making
33: Interpersonal Competence

Collaborative Writers, Round One: Word Wizards

Time: 5–8 minutes

You Will Need: Alphabet cards, timer

Break the group into small teams of four to eight. Give each group a stack of alphabet cards. The group will play against the clock for 2–3 minutes (use an egg timer or a stopwatch). During that time, each team should use their cards to create one word that will serve as a crossword puzzle–type base. If they get the base word created before time is out, they can then build new words that extend out from any of its letters.

Select one person from each team to start by drawing the first card from the deck and laying it face up. The next person should draw the second card and add to the first letter, with the goal of creating a word. If the second team member doesn't think the drawn letter will create a word (for example, the first letter drawn is a *B* and the next letter is a *Z*), he should discard the letter into a pile, face down, and the next person should draw. Team members should continue taking turns, forming as many words as they can until time is up.

Recognize the teams who completed words, used the most letters, used unique letters (like *Z, Q, V, X*), created the most words, created the largest word, and created the shortest word.

Collaborative Writers, Round Two: Sentence Starters

Time: 5 minutes

After playing the previous game, have the teams use the word or words they created to craft as many sentences as they can in three minutes. When time is up, go around to each group and have them share their sentences. Have the players vote on their favorite sentence.

Collaborative Writers, Round Three: Story Stacks

Time: 10–20 minutes

Write on chart paper two or three of the entire group's favorite sentences. Then challenge each team to create a short story that includes the two or three favorite sentences. Give the teams 5–10 minutes to write their stories, and, again, have each group share their tale. (If you don't have 5–10 minutes of group time left, simply have them tell the story out loud instead of writing it down.)

Let's Talk

- What happened in the first game? The second? The third?

- Was there anything hard you had to learn during these games? What did you learn?

- What helped you and your team play this game well together?

- Next time, how would you play differently?

- What else would you like to learn to do?

Focus on Assets

16: High Expectations
21: Achievement Motivation
32: Planning and Decision Making
33: Interpersonal Competence

By the Roll

Time: 5–15 minutes

You Will Need: One die per team, one sheet of paper and pen per player

Break the group into small teams of six. Explain that players will take turns rolling the die. If a player rolls a six, she should grab a pen and start writing on her paper, using one of the preset tasks below or a task of your own creation.

Players should continue to take turns rolling the die until the next person rolls a six. At that point, the new person should grab a pen and start writing on his own paper while the previous person puts down her pen. Each player who rolls a six will try to complete her writing task before she must put down the pen. Continue to rotate pen use based on whoever rolls a six. The first person to finish the task accurately wins. Speed and accuracy are of the essence.

Possible writing tasks:

- Write letters in all caps from A to Z (for more of a challenge, write all letters in caps from A to Z, then write all letters in lowercase letters from A to Z).

- Write down the numbers from 1 to 100.

- Write down the numbers from 1,000 to 5,000 by 10s (3rd grade).

For the following, you may want to put the starting point on the children's papers (for example, 1 x 1 = 1, 1 + 1 = 2):

- Do your times tables: ones, twos (or whatever number you're working on).

- Add the number one to each answer:
  $1 + 1 = 2 + 1 = 3 + 1 = 4 + 1 = 5$.

- Keep subtracting the number one from each answer (work backward):
  $50 - 1 = 49 - 1 = 48 - 1 = 47$.

Let's Talk

- Did using dice make you want to do a good job? What makes you want to do a good job in school?

- Did playing against others make the game more fun or harder? What can you do when hard things happen in your life?

- Why is it important to work hard in school?

Focus on Assets

16: High Expectations
21: Achievement Motivation
22: School Engagement

Story Perspectives

Time: 15–30 minutes

You Will Need: Paper, pencils

Prep with Children: Talk about adjectives. Explain what they are and give examples. Make sure everyone understands the examples you give.

Break players into teams of three. Have each group choose a random item from the room to be an "object of interest." Instruct team members to arrange themselves around the object so that each person is looking at it from a different angle. For example, if the object is a glass, one player may stand over the glass, looking down at it. Another player may place herself eye level with the glass, pressing her nose against its side. Another might sit on the floor and look up at the glass.

Have players keep their perspective for one minute. Ask: *What does the object look like from where you are? Can you feel the object from where you are sitting or standing? Can you hear it? Does it have a smell?*

After one minute, have the players silently reflect on their observations and write down two adjectives to describe the object from their perspective. If they need a reminder about adjectives, prompt them with one or two. Once they are finished, have players share their adjectives with their teammates and discuss what they saw, heard, or smelled from their perspective. Next, have each team create a story or poem about their object, using the adjectives they came up with as well as their individual perspectives.

Let children share their object and poem or story creation in a show-and-tell. Help them by giving them a format to follow: Introduce the object, tell the group what they noticed about it, and read the story or poem.

If there is enough time, have players look at their object again, this time changing perspectives to see if they gain new observations other than those already mentioned. Allow one to two minutes for conversation.

Let's Talk

- Why do you think people think of the same thing in different ways?

- Why should we listen carefully to others? How does it help us understand each other better?

- Why is it good to have different kinds of friends? How might it make you a stronger person?

If you want to go deeper with varying perspectives, you could pair this activity with the book *The True Story of the Three Little Pigs* by Jon Scieszka. See page 107.

Focus on Assets

17: Creative Activities
33: Interpersonal Competence
34: Cultural Competence

Portable Words

Time: 5–15 minutes

You Will Need: Index cards with one random word on each card, enough for everyone in the class (or refrigerator word magnets).

Spread the words out on a table. Divide players into teams and have them create a television ad (or a story or poem) using as many of the words as possible. To add meaning to the activity, give children a theme to work around, such as friends or things they do for fun.

Variation: Turn this into a fast game with competitive rounds: Each person grabs one word from the table. The players then hurry to mingle with each other to see who can match their word with another to form a word pair first. For example: *red* and *dress* for *red dress.*

Let's Talk

• What helped you be creative in this activity?

• Why is it important to be creative?

• What is something you care a lot about that should be in a TV commercial?

• Why do you care so much about it?

• If you could wear a sign that says something about you, what would the sign say?

Focus on Assets
17: Creative Activities
28: Integrity
37: Personal Power

Impromptu Authors

Time: 10–20 minutes

You Will Need: Paper, pencils, homemade books containing blank pages and covers (optional). See page 102 for instructions on making a book.

Ask several players to give you random words off the top of their head. List them on a whiteboard or butcher paper. Have each person write a story that includes all the listed words. Ask for volunteers to read their story aloud, or have the players write their story and draw pictures in a homemade book. Players can exchange books to read.

Variation 1: Ask for volunteers to make up a story out loud, using all the words given.

Variation 2: Break the larger group into teams, and have them create a story using all the words and adding pictures to illustrate the story.

Let's Talk

• Are you able to do something right away when someone tells you to? Is that hard or fun?

• How did you choose the story you made up with the words I gave you?

• If you could tell a story about your life, what would it be about?

• What do you want to have happen later in your life that would make a fun story?

Focus on Assets
37: Personal Power
40: Positive View of Personal Future

Build a Body

Time: 5–15 minutes

You Will Need: Chalkboard, paper or chart paper, and writing instrument

This game is a reversed version of Hangman. The goal is to *build* a person rather than *hang* one. Have each player quietly come up with one or two words. Instruct the children to keep their word(s) to themselves. Pick someone to go first as the game leader. The game leader should tell the group how many letters her word has and draw a blank for each letter on the board (or on paper if you break the group into smaller teams that play together around a table). Children can guess letters, and as they're guessed correctly, the leader can fill them in the appropriate blank. After a letter is correctly guessed, the game leader should also draw part of the person (e.g., head, arm, leg). Have the leader keep a list of incorrect letters on the board as those are called out, too. Challenge players to guess fewer incorrect letters in the next round of play.

Variation: Before the game begins, make body parts out of paper or felt. (Draw the body first, then cut it into separate pieces, and add tape or Velcro to the back of each body part.) When a correct letter is called out, the player who guessed it should select a body part and place it on the board or piece of cloth. With each correct guess, the body will slowly come together.

Let's Talk

• How many guesses did it take to build a person?

• We built this person together. What else can we do when we work together?

• How can we support one another, or build each other up, with our words?

• What are things we can do to help someone have a good day?

Focus on Assets
26: Caring
32: Planning and Decision Making
33: Interpersonal Competence
37: Personal Power

FOLLOW THE LEADER GAMES

Red Light, Green Light

Time: 10–20 minutes

You Will Need: Red and green dots

This is an oldie but goodie with a new twist. First, select one person to be the "light" and instruct him to stand at one end of your playing area, with his back to the other children. All the other players should stand at the opposite end. Tell them the object of the game is to be the first person to tag the light. The light will direct the players' movements by whipping around periodically to call out either "red light" or "green light." When "red light" is called, everyone must freeze and stay where they are. If they move, and the light catches them, they're out. When "green light" is called, everyone should walk quickly toward the light, keeping in mind the light could call out "red light" at any time.

Here's what's new: Give red dots to the players who are caught moving during a red light, and green dots to those who stayed put. Keep going until the light is tagged, and declare the winner the new light. Play a couple of rounds and have players keep their dots.

Let's Talk

• After the game, sit down to discuss the "lights" (individual behavior, rules, boundaries, and expectations) of the classroom, entire school, place of faith, or program. Red lights are stoplights—the "no" rules. Green lights mean go—the "yes" rules.

- For each red dot, have each player share one "red light" rule for the classroom or program (for example, no talking during rest time, no fighting, no cursing).

- For each green dot, have players share a "green light" rule for the classroom or program (for example, getting permission to go to the bathroom, saying "please" and "thank you," treating each other nicely).

Note: To shorten time, have a few players talk about their dots, instead of each player talking about each dot she has.

Focus on Assets
10: Safety
12: School Boundaries
16: High Expectations

Bubble Gum Light

Time: 5 minutes

You Will Need: Bubble gum

See instructions for the "light" in Red Light, Green Light, above.

As a fun treat or energy builder, distribute bubble gum to all players. Have one person be the light. With each green light, players should try to blow the biggest bubble possible and maintain it. When the light says "red light" and turns around, everyone should stop blowing their bubble, and the red light will declare who has the biggest bubble. The winner becomes the light for the next round. Play as many rounds as is fun or as time allows.

Let's Talk

- What is something you want to do that's really big, like a bubble? How can you do this really big thing?

- Have you ever done something good that no one else saw? Are you glad you did it even if no one saw you do it?

- Why is it important to do the right thing even when no one sees it?

Focus on Assets
16: High Expectations
28: Integrity

Teacher Says

Time: 5–10 minutes

An adaptation of Simon Says, this game helps teach players to follow directions (could also be Mommy Says, Daddy Says, Coach Says, and so on).

Here are the rules: The leader stands before the group and calls out instructions for the group to follow. Players are to follow Teacher's instructions when he starts with the phrase "Teacher says." But if the leader simply says something like "Pat your belly" and a player pats her belly, then she's out because the leader didn't say "Teacher says" before "Pat your belly." The leader's objective is to catch as many players following instructions at the wrong time. To prompt this to happen, he will state the orders and demonstrate the motions quickly. The last person or last few people left in the game win.

Let's Talk
Have a conversation about rules and why it's important for children to follow them. Ask the following questions. Make sure the discussion points out the importance of safety, playing fair, and learning responsibility.

- What are the rules we have for our classroom (or home, team, or program)?

- Which rules do you understand? Which rules do you not understand?

- Which rules do you like? Why?

- Which rules do you not like? Why?

- Why do we have rules?

Consider reading *Miss Nelson Is Missing!* by Harry Allard when you play this game. Find out more on page 73.

Focus on Assets
5: Caring School Climate
12: School Boundaries
31: Self-Regulation

Follow the Leader

Time: 5–10 minutes

Designate a leader. All players should mimic the leader's actions. Repeat as often as you want.

Let's Talk

- Have you ever had people follow your lead in doing something?

- Have you ever helped someone or talked someone into doing a good thing? What did you do? What happened?

- Have you ever talked someone into doing something you knew you shouldn't do? What happened?

- How can you be a good leader at home? At school? In your neighborhood?

Focus on Assets
8: Children as Resources
15: Positive Peer Influence
30: Responsibility
39: Sense of Purpose

Contrary Leaders

Time: 5–10 minutes

In this game, a twist on Follow the Leader, it's OK to do something contrary or even funny, in comparison to what the leader does. Instead of following the leader's actions, the players should do the *opposite* of the leader's actions. For example, if the leader reaches his hands up to the sky, the children would bend over to touch their toes.

Let's Talk

- What happens when you do the opposite of what your mom or dad wants you to do? How about when you do the opposite of what your teacher asks?

- Why is it important to follow their rules and instructions?

- Is there ever a time when it might be OK to do the opposite of what someone tells you? What times would those be? What if a grown-up wanted you to do something wrong or mean? What could you do?

Focus on Assets
11: Family Boundaries
12: School Boundaries
28: Integrity
35: Resistance Skills

The Review Line Game

Time: 5–15 minutes

You Will Need: A prepared list of review questions that cover a subject the children have been learning about

Divide the children into two lines, and ask the two line leaders a review question. The two children can shout out their answers. The first one to answer correctly should stay in place, and the one who answered incorrectly or not quickly enough should move to the back of the line. The children in that line then move up, creating a new line leader. Ask another review question and repeat the process.

Note: You may have to set a boundary before the game begins to keep one person from answering all the questions. At the outset of the game, state that if someone answers five questions correctly, remaining their line's leader, that person will move to the teacher's table to help you pick out the next question.

Let's Talk

• Do you learn better when you're being active or when you're sitting still?

• Do you learn better by yourself or with others?

• What do you like to learn about the most?

Focus on Assets
16: High Expectations
21: Achievement Motivation
22: School Engagement

Space Travel

Time: 5–10 minutes

Sit in a circle, and set the scene by saying: *I'm packing things in a spaceship to travel through time. I need to take apples, bandages, and cups.* Turn to the person next to you, and tell her to repeat the items you just said plus a new item. Continue around the circle until everyone has had a turn.

Let's Talk

• How did you think of things you would need to take on the spaceship?

• How do you plan for daily activities or trips in real life?

• How did you remember all the items that everyone wanted to take on the spaceship?

• How do you remember facts and information needed at school, at home, or in other activities?

Focus on Assets
32: Planning and Decision Making
37: Personal Power

ARTSY GAMES

Collaborative Song Writers

Time: 5–15 minutes

You Will Need: Paper, pencils

In teams, rewrite well-known seasonal songs to fit another season or kind of weather. Unless you are working in a religious setting, make sure not to use songs that mention a religious holiday, such as Christmas or Hanukkah, to avoid leaving any children out. Two good songs to start with are "Jingle Bells" and "Let It Snow." For example, children can change the lyrics of "Jingle Bells" to

something like "Sand and Shells" to reflect summer and the lyrics of "Let It Snow" to "Rain and Blow" to fit a thunderstorm theme. You can also start with simpler songs they might know, such as the "ABC Song" or "I Love You" (the Barney song).

Sample progression: First, help the group learn one song or poem by repeating it until they all know it by heart. Next, use that particular tune or poem for every rewrite that you do—think of it as a song or poem for all seasons.

Variation: Use familiar nursery rhymes or poems instead of songs to pattern the students' creative works (for example, "Old Mother Hubbard" or "Jack and Jill").

Let's Talk

• Do you like doing activities like this by yourself, or do you like to work with others?

• How did your group use everyone's skills, the things they are really good at? Did everyone have a chance to help?

• What are some things you can do to make working in a group easier or better?

Focus on Assets
17: Creative Activities
33: Interpersonal Competence

Superheroes Live and in Action!

Time: 5–20 minutes

Have children come up with a list of situations they face that call for positive action (for example, someone is new at school, a room is full of trash, someone is crying and sad). Divide the group into acting troupes. Have them act out the various scenarios, showing how they can be heroes in each situation. After each scene, talk about the situation and how each person thinks he could be a hero in it. Brainstorm ideas.

This can be done as a one-time activity or can be broken into multiple acts to emphasize over time a theme of responsibility, caring, and respect. Try Superhero Fridays—have the children act out a scenario and then find a way to engage in superhero service around the school, house, or program site.

Variation: Play this game like charades. Let one acting troupe role-play while the other team tries to guess what the first group is acting out.

Let's Talk

• How can we show caring every day?

• How can we be nice to others through what we do?

• How can we take care of the earth by what we do?

• Which situation was the hardest one to be a superhero in? Why? Who could help you in a situation like that? What else could you do?

Consider reading *Flat Stanley* by Jeff Brown and Scott Nash after you play this game. Find out more on page 90.

Focus on Assets
8: Children as Resources
9: Service to Others
26: Caring

Human Band

Time: 5–10 minutes

Break the group into three sections: drummers, backup clappers, and singers. The drummers will stomp their feet, the clappers will clap their hands, and the singers will hum. Have the group choose a song they want to practice (one that they all know). On your signal, each section will keep time and perform to the beat. Fade a section in or out at your discretion. Have the children practice holding notes, and if it is going well, consider having one group perform solo. Finish big or finish melodically—it's up to you. If you have time, allow musicians to switch roles.

Let's Talk

• Why is the conductor an important part of the band? What happens if one band member ignores the conductor?

- What other "instruments" could be added to the band? (If time permits, try the song with the newly added human band instruments.)

- What real instrument would you like to play?

- What is your favorite song? What do you like about it?

- Is there a song that cheers you up when you're sad? What is it? What about a song you listen to when you're mad?

After playing this game, you might consider reading *Mole Music* by David McPhail. See more about this book on page 74.

Focus on Assets
17: Creative Activities

Back Drawings

Time: 10–20 minutes

You Will Need: Paper, crayons or pencils, tape

Each player should draw a picture from a category that you provide, such as food, animals, superheroes, and so on. Give children 5–10 minutes to draw. After they're finished, ask a volunteer to be the "easel" and stand with his back toward the class. Select an artist to come to the front of the room and without showing the easel her artwork, tape it to the easel's back. The children viewing the exhibit should describe the piece to help the easel guess what the picture is of.

Let's Talk

Explain to the children that we can only know things through our own perceptions.

- What if only one person could see the art on the easel? How would the others know what it looked like?

- What can we learn by listening to each other? How does listening to others help us make friends?

Pair with John Godfrey Saxe's version of *The Blind Men and the Elephant,* a tale about six blind brothers who each have a different perspective of an elephant they stumble upon. Each man touches a different part of the elephant and describes what he feels. The brothers argue long and hard over what the elephant looks like. The moral is that all the pieces have to be put together to figure out what is real.

Focus on Assets
17: Creative Activities

An Artist's Tale

Time: 30 minutes

You Will Need: Paper, pencils or crayons, a pre-made list of 10 items to draw (for example: *pig, car, bear, mountain, dinosaur, tree, penguin, backpack, basketball, flower*)

If you have a large group, break it into smaller groups of 10 and have the children sit in a circle. Put one piece of paper in front of each player. Call out the first item for the children to draw. Give them a couple of minutes to draw, then say, "Switch," which means each child should hand his piece of paper to the person on his right. Call out the second item for them to draw on the new piece of paper in front of them. Have the children keep rotating the papers and drawing new pictures until they end up one paper short of their original drawing. (You don't want them to end up with the one they started with.) Each player should then tell a story based on the drawings on his paper.

Note: For children in grades K–1, read the first item from the list and have them start drawing it. Wait a minute or two. Then call out the second object to draw. Let the children know that it's OK if they don't finish the first picture before they move to the next.

Let's Talk

- Look at your group art piece. How does each picture add to the whole piece? What does each person in the class add to the classroom?

- Look at all the art pieces. How are they different? How are they the same?

- How are we different? How are we the same?

- What do you think makes you special?

Pair this activity with the books *The Dot* on page 65 or *Ish* on page 71, both by Peter H. Reynolds.

Focus on Assets
17: Creative Activities
34: Cultural Competence
38: Self-Esteem

Hidden Treasures

Time: 5–10 minutes

You Will Need: A couple of ordinary objects like a pen, paper clip, or hair ribbon

Sit in a circle. Hand a pen to the person next to you and say, *This may look like an ordinary pen, but it's really a (sword, alien, tie).* That person should take the pen, make the same starting statement ("This may look like an ordinary pen, but it's really a . . .") and finish with what she thinks it *really* is. Have the

children continue to p̶ whole circle until the̶ until you're back to ̶ Take the next obje̶

Let's Talk

- Finish this sentence: *People look at ̶ say I'm an ordinary kid, but I'm* really a . . .

- How would you finish this sentence? *Others say this is* just *a math class, but it's really important because . . .*

- What would you say if someone said to you, *It would be OK to take that bubble gum from the store—it's* just *a piece of bubble gum?*

- Why is it important to be honest, even about little things?

Focus on Assets
29: Honesty
37: Personal Power
38: Self-Esteem

Alphabet Pictures

Time: 5–10 minutes

You Will Need: Paper, pencils

Distribute paper and pencils, and have all players draw an *A* on the middle of their papers. Challenge them to use the *A* as a base for a picture. Say: *When you look at the* A *what do you see?* Encourage them to turn their paper around and look at the letter from different angles. If they get stuck, give them an example: an *A* could become a wizard cap, an *L* could become a box. Use as many letters as you have time for, or try simple words like *mom* so the children can create larger images. At the end, have children share their drawings.

Let's Talk

- What new things did you see with each letter?

...ers shared their drawings, did you ...k of new pictures to draw? What ...re they?

If you squint your eyes and stare at your picture, what do you see?

- Art is about seeing possibilities, what *could be*. Do you have dreams for your life? What would you like to be when you grow up? What would you like to do? Where would you like to go?

- What can you do to make one of your dreams come true? (Save money for a trip? Join a basketball team to learn how to play? Study hard in math and science to become a doctor?)

This activity pairs well with *The Turn-Around, Upside-Down Alphabet Book* by Lisa Campbell Ernst. See page 81 for more details.

Focus on Assets
32: Planning and Decision Making
37: Personal Power
39: Sense of Purpose
40: Positive View of Personal Future

Animal Charades

Time: 5–15 minutes

Ask children to think of an animal they like. Tell them to close their eyes and think about what that animal smells, looks, and sounds like. Direct them to think about what it eats and what it looks like when it's running or trying to move fast. After a few minutes, ask for volunteers to come up before the group and take turns silently acting out their animal. Tell them they cannot make any animal sounds such as growls, meows, or hisses. Let the rest of the group guess what animal is being portrayed.

Expand the game: After playing this game, give the children time to draw their animals.

Variation: After all the players have chosen their animal, have them mimic their animal and roam around to see if they find any other animals just like theirs.

Let's Talk

- What animal did you want to be? Why?

- Can you think of a person you want to be like? Who is it?

- What do you like about that person?

- Do you think that if you're nice, other people will see that and want to be nice too?

Consider reading *Danny and the Dinosaur* by Syd Hoff when you play this game. Find out more on page 89.

Focus on Assets
14: Adult Role Models
15: Positive Peer Influence
26: Caring

Workout Rolls

Time: 5 minutes or less

You Will Need: One die

Roll the die and have the group do a different physical activity for each number rolled (see below). The goal is to get the group through all six numbers.

- 1: Stretch up on your tiptoes and raise your hands as high as you can.
- 2: Stretch your neck by leaning your head to the right and then to the left.
- 3: Do three knee bends.
- 4: Shrug your shoulders up and down four times.
- 5: Bend over and touch your toes five times.
- 6: Lie on the floor and do six sit-ups.

Let's Talk

- Why is it important to exercise?
- Why do you think exercise helps us when we feel sad, mad, or bored?
- How can you make exercise a part of each day?
- What else can you do to take care of yourself?

Focus on Assets
31: Self-Regulation
37: Personal Power

Cinderella's Shoes

Time: 5 minutes

You Will Need: A copy of the book *Cinderella*

Form a circle of chairs and sit down to read *Cinderella* aloud. After you have read the book, instruct children to form pairs. One child in each pair will be Cinderella and one will be the prince. Have all the Cinderellas take off their shoes and pile them in the center of the circle and then return to their seat. Ask the princes to turn around, so they are looking at the Cinderellas and not at the shoes in the circle. Mix up all the shoes. Tell them that when you give the alert that midnight is striking, each prince should scramble to find his Cinderella's shoes, race back to her, and help her put on the shoes. If they grab the wrong pair, they should return to the pile—without hints or help from their Cinderella—to try again. The first Cinderella/ prince pair to find and put on the right shoes wins the rights to living happily ever after!

Let's Talk

- Who has helped you do something before?
- Has anyone ever helped you get out of something bad? How did this person help you?
- Have you ever helped someone else get out of something bad?
- How does it feel when you help another person?

Focus on Assets
26: Caring
39: Sense of Purpose

Clang Clang

Time: 5 minutes

You Will Need: A barrier (a door, cart with a sheet, chalkboard), an aluminum pie pan, an assortment of 10 small, unbreakable objects to drop into the pie pan (penny, jacks, beanbag, spoon), a pen and sheet of paper for each person

Gather your 10 unbreakable items, and set up the barrier. Give the children a chance to see the items so they have *some* idea of what is being dropped out of sight. Then, give each player a pen and paper, and ask them to number their paper from 1 to 10. From behind the barrier, drop the items one at a time into the pie tin. The objects will create different sounds as they fall against the metal surface. As items are dropped, children should try to guess what each one is, and write it down next to the corresponding number on their paper.

Let's Talk

• How did you use your sense of hearing to guess what was dropped in the tin?

• Most people have five senses—hearing, smelling, seeing, touching, and tasting. How do your senses help you during the day?

• Did you pay attention while I dropped an item into the tin? Did it help you guess?

• How does paying attention help you at school, at home, or while playing sports?

Focus on Assets
21: Achievement Motivation
37: Personal Power

Guessing Game

Time: 5 minutes

You Will Need: A paper bag, several random objects for guessing (try to find items that could be easily confused with two or more other objects)

Put one of the objects in a paper bag and let one child at a time reach into the bag to feel the object. If no one guesses correctly the first time around, offer clues to help them guess. For example, if an apple is in the bag, you might say, "It keeps the doctor away" or "It can be gold, green, or red." Once someone guesses correctly, switch to another object and let the group try again.

Variation: Fill small paper cups with a random assortment of scented objects (e.g., soap, grass, flowers, an orange). Blindfold players, and then go around the circle to see who can guess the item in each cup.

Let's Talk

• Most people have five senses—we can see, hear, smell, touch, and taste. How did you use your senses to guess what was in the bag?

• Did you make a quick guess or did you take your time to figure out what was inside the bag?

• Do you make quick guesses about people you meet, or do you really get to know someone before you decide if you like that person or not?

• What can you do to get to know other kids in your neighborhood or at school?

Focus on Assets
4: Caring Neighborhood
5: Caring School Climate
34: Cultural Competence

Spy Masters

Time: 5–15 minutes

You Will Need: A pre-generated list of items (see examples below), index cards

Preparation: Create a list of objects for players to "spy." List one object on each index card to create a deck of cards.

Have one person pull out a card and read it aloud. (Read it aloud yourself if children cannot yet read.) The first player to find (that is, "spy") something in the room that relates to the item on the index card should raise his hand, point to the thing he spied, and explain how it relates to the item written on the card.

Note: Children should share how their object relates to the phrase on the card because it may not be obvious to others. For example, if the card says "A food I like to eat," and there isn't food in the room, a player may point to a *picture* that has food in it. Or, a player may point to trash on the floor when she draws a card that asks how the room could be made a better place and then explain that she means by picking up the trash.

If the group doesn't see the connection (if they don't agree), give the players a chance to raise their hand and try again for that same card. You might also let several players answer for each "Spy Masters" to extend the game and include more children. Have the player who "spied" something first draw the next card to read aloud and continue play.

Spy Masters Examples:

- My favorite book
- Someone I can talk to when I'm sad or angry
- A game I like to play
- A food I enjoy eating
- Someone who cares about me
- A friend I like to play with
- Someone who helps me with my schoolwork
- A school rule I like
- A rule I have at home
- A rule at home that I like
- Something that keeps me safe
- A subject I'm good at
- An activity I'm good at
- A school or home rule that keeps me safe
- Something I'd like to do when I grow up
- A place I'd like to visit
- A food I'd like to try
- Someone I care about
- A chore I can do for myself
- Something I made myself (a picture, craft project, poem)
- An instrument I can play or would like to play
- Something that makes me feel less afraid when I'm scared
- Something I can do to make this a better/safer/cleaner place
- Someone I know outside of school
- Someone who was nice to someone else today
- Someone who shared
- Someone who helped the teacher during class
- A sport I like to play

Let's Talk

- Was this game easy or hard for you? Why?
- Why is it important to learn to look for things, even when they are hard to find? How will that skill help you in life?

- What should you do when you "spy" your friends making smart choices and being nice and responsible?

- What do you like people to do or say when they "spy" you doing good things?

- Why should we do good things?

Consider reading *Walking through the Jungle* by Julie Lacome when you play this game. Find out more on page 82.

Focus on Assets
15: Positive Peer Influence
28: Integrity
30: Responsibility

TEAM-BUILDING GAMES

Superhero Team Relay

Time: 20–30 minutes

You Will Need: Two purses, two capes and two masks (optional), chairs (four to eight per "downtown" setup—see below), two to four tables per group, two blankets, two stuffed kittens, six volunteers (who can rotate in and out, so they can take their turn in the relay)

Set up your playing area with an obstacle course that supports any book you're reading about superheroes. Feel free to adapt the course to follow the book's scenario.

Preparation/Course Setup: Set up two identical obstacle course layouts. The first part of the obstacle course represents a downtown area of streets and alleys and can be set up using chairs that dead-end into a wall or some other large object. The second part of the course is simply set by using one or two tables that the superhero can crawl under. Each course should have a dark alley where superheroes can change into their costumes. You can create this alley by draping down a blanket that children can run behind to make their quick change. Place one costume (mask and cape) in each alley. (For the capes, use a shawl or scarf that can easily be tied around the neck or cheap plastic Halloween capes.)

For a more economical version, simply have the children make circles with their index fingers and thumbs and hold them up over their eyes as pretend masks, and skip the costumes altogether.)

Next, gather the volunteers and individually go over their roles as victim, thief, or veterinarian. Explain that the victim starts off the story by calling for help and explaining to the superhero how he was robbed, pointing the hero toward the thief. The thief's role is to respond in character to the superhero's lecture when caught and act apologetic and grateful for the second chance. The vet simply helps when needed. Explain to all the volunteers that they will need to reset their objects (the thief's stolen purse, the vet's kitten patient) at the end of each round of the relay.

Then help each volunteer find her place along the course. The victim volunteer should stand near the starting point. Further down, at the dead end, should be the volunteer thief holding the victim's purse. The veterinarian volunteer should stand near the second part of the obstacle course, prepared to help when needed. Explain to all the children what the superhero's role is, how to run the course, and how she should interact with each volunteer player along the way. You may want to demonstrate how to navigate the course and what each superhero is expected to do along the route.

Relay Directions: Ask the volunteers and other participants if they have questions and make any necessary clarifications. Cue the volunteer victims to start calling for help to begin the race. Once the first superheros on each relay team hears the call for help from the victim, he races to his team's alley to put on his costume. (If you are using the economical version, this can be simulated by the heroes simply turning their backs to everyone and then whipping around with their pretend masks in place.)

Next, the two competing heroes run toward their team's victim, who explains the purse-snatching and points the hero in the thief's direction. Each hero chases the thief by running through the downtown area, which means going around the chairs set in the obstacle course. The hero catches the thief, who is standing at the dead end looking around for a way out. The hero lectures the thief about being good from here on out and taking advantage of the opportunity the hero is giving him to go straight. The hero gets the purse and returns through downtown to give the purse back to its grateful owner. The victim then tells the hero that a kitten just fell into the sewer drain and begs the superhero to save it. The superhero crawls through the sewer drain by crawling under the table(s) to retrieve the kitten. Once the kitten is retrieved, the superhero crawls out on the other side, races the animal to the vet for care, and then quickly returns to the alley to change back into street clothes and race back to tag the next person in line. The next superhero repeats the course and so on until there is a winning superhero team.

Note: Teams can also be awarded points for superheroes who give the best speech, respond to the victim in the kindest way, and interact well with the veterinarian.

Let's Talk

- How were you a superhero? How did you help others?

- Have you ever helped someone out at school, at home, or in your neighborhood? How?

- What values do you think superheroes have?

- What values do you have? Is it important to care about others? To tell the truth? Not to steal?

- Have you ever done something wrong and had someone give you a chance to make things right? How did that feel?

Consider reading *Flat Stanley* by Jeff Brown and Scott Nash when you play this game. Find out more on page 90.

Focus on Assets
9: Service to Others
26: Caring
30: Responsibility
37: Personal Power

Stack-Up Cups

Time: 10–15 minutes

You Will Need: Two sets of 10 cups, a table

Divide players into two teams. Set up competition in one of two ways: (1) against each other in a relay-race format or (2) against the clock (the best combined time of all the rounds wins).

Note: This second variation requires keeping track of times and recording them. At the end, it builds in the opportunity to practice some math skills for determining the best overall time and the winning team.

Players line up at one end of the room. On the word *go,* the first player from each team runs to the opposite end of the room where the cups are placed on top of a table. Each person stacks his cups in pyramid fashion, then unstacks them, and yells "Done" when finished. For Version 1, have players run back when finished, and tag the next player in line. For Version 2, stop the clock to record times. After determining the winning team, debrief the group by noting that the game is all about "ups" and "downs."

Let's Talk

Ask players to talk about the up and down parts of their day:

- What has gone well today? What have you enjoyed? What have you done that you're proud of?

- What hasn't gone well today? What have you had a hard time with? Have you needed help or encouragement with something? If yes, what?

- What helps you turn a down into an up? What helps you when you are sad, afraid, mad, or hurt?

- How can you support one another through the ups and downs in life?

Focus on Assets
37: Personal Power
38: Self-Esteem
39: Sense of Purpose
40: Positive View of Personal Future

Tug of War

Time: 5–10 minutes

You Will Need: Gaffer tape or something else to make temporary lines on the floor, rope with a bandanna tied to the middle of it

Mark two lines on the floor, 10 steps apart. The rope's mid-point with the bandanna tied to it should be in the middle of the marked-off space. Divide the group into two teams and give them a minute or two to situate themselves. Have them pick up each end of the rope. On "go," each team should try to pull its side of the rope past the nearest line. The team that pulls the bandanna past its line wins.

Let's Talk

- Just like you tugged on the rope, have you ever had someone tug at you to try to get you to do something you didn't want to do?

- Peer pressure can be positive or negative. It's good when friends try to get us to do good things, like help others, do our homework, or play during recess. What are some good things your friends talk you into doing?

- Peer pressure is negative when friends or classmates try to get you to do something wrong or bad, like cheat on a test, get into a fight, or make fun of someone. What are some bad things that others have tried to get you to do?

- What can you do to fight off the negative tugs of others?

- What can you do to help tug others to do good?

Focus on Assets
28: Integrity
30: Responsibility
35: Resistance Skills
36: Peaceful Conflict Resolution

Group Roll

Time: 10–15 minutes

You Will Need: A ball

Have the group form a circle. Have children stand with their feet spread apart, bent over with their hands reaching toward their toes, but with heads up so that they can see around the circle. One person starts with the ball and rolls it to someone else in the circle. The object is to keep the ball within the circle and not let it roll out of the circle through someone's legs. If the ball escapes through someone's legs, then that player has to say something positive or nice about himself. If he can't think of anything, he turns his back to the circle. He becomes part of the circle again if someone else deliberately rolls the ball through his legs and says something nice about him.

Let's Talk

- How easy was it to think of something good to say about yourself?

- What helps you feel good about yourself?

- How did it feel to hear other players say something nice about you?

- How often do you point out good things about others?

- Do you think it's a good idea to say positive things about others? Why or why not?

Focus on Assets
15: Positive Peer Influence
38: Self-Esteem
39: Sense of Purpose

Balloon Keep-Up

Time: 5–10 minutes

You Will Need: Balloons, a watch with a second hand or a stopwatch

Have the children form small circles of 6–10 students each and join hands. Toss one balloon into each group and challenge them to keep it in the air for as long as possible without letting it touch the ground. Time rounds and record each team's personal best.

Variation: Instead of using a watch to time the groups, have them see how high they can

count by counting out loud while they keep the balloon in the air.

Variation: Have the players form one large group and use one beach ball instead of balloons.

Let's Talk

- We kept track of personal bests. What is something you want to do your best at? What can you do to make that happen?

- How did your team work together?

- Did you talk to each other and help each other out? How?

- Why is it important to work together?

Focus on Assets
33: Interpersonal Competence

Beep Beep!

Time: 5–15 minutes

Gather into a circle. Ask the group to share what noises a car makes. Share with them the three key car noises (if not already shared) that will be used in this game: *varoom*—for starting up a car engine, *beep beep*—for the horn, and *errrr*—for the car's brakes. Let them practice all three sounds with you. Pick a person to start the car and say "Varoom." Then have the player next to her hit the horn and say "Beep, beep." Then instruct the player next to her in the circle to hit the brakes and say "Errrr!" Continue the sequence all the way around the circle. Keep repeating the sequence, but speed it up each round to see if children can keep the sequence going without messing up. If someone makes a mistake, then that person is skipped the next time around.

Let's Talk

- People honk the horn in their car as a warning to keep people safe. Are there times when you need to warn people to keep them safe? How do you do that?

- Sometimes people need to slam on their brakes when they're driving, to keep someone safe. Are there times when you need to stop doing something that isn't safe?

Focus on Assets
10: Safety
30: Responsibility
32: Planning and Decision Making

Station Relay

Time: 10–12 minutes

Instead of the usual relay race, set up four stations in sequential order in the corners of the play area. Divide the group into teams of four. Let each team member choose a station and stand in the appropriate corner. Then give station directions:

- At the first station, Player 1 from each team will do 10 jumping jacks, then run to the second station and tag Player 2, who will then do 10 push-ups.

- Upon completion of her push-ups, Player 2 runs to station three to tag Player 3.

- Player 3 does 10 sit-ups, then runs to the next station and tags Player 4.

- Player 4 does 15 squats and then runs to station one to complete the relay.

Let's Talk

- How did it feel to be part of a team?

- What did your team do well?

- How did the people on your team help each other? How can you help your friends every day?

- What can you do to be healthy and strong?

Focus on Assets
31: Self-Regulation
37: Personal Power
38: Self-Esteem

BACKWARD PLAY

Note: All of the games in this section should be scored backward, with the winner being the last one to complete the activity. Don't tell the participants how they will be scored until *after* the activity—otherwise, the game could last a lot longer than you anticipated!

Animal Match

Time: 5–10 minutes

You Will Need: Pre-generated index card sets

Preparation: Create two-card "animal and animal sound" sets: The first card of each set should be an animal card with either a picture or the name of that animal on it. The second card of the set should feature the sound that animal makes, only written backward. (For example, the cat card would have a matching card with "woem" written on it.) To help

the children out, you may want to write the actual sound (e.g., "meow") in smaller print underneath the backward sound.

Distribute one animal or one sound card to each child. (Make sure to pass these out so that there are enough of each to make matching sets.) Have the animals and sounds try to find each other. Those with the sound cards wander around and ask others, "Does your animal go [player makes their backward sound]?" The animal should reply no, if it's not her animal. If it is, she should say something like "A cat doesn't say woem! It says meow!" To which the "woem" card holder replies, "Oh, I had it backward. Meow." And the two sit down together. The last group to match up gets a point. (Remember—it's backward!)

Let's Talk

- In this game you had to notice when something was wrong and make it right. Do you ever see things that are wrong (trash on the floor, bullying)? What can you do to make them right?

- Think of a time when you did something wrong. How did you find out you made a mistake?

- In this game the team who finished last was the winner. Was that fair?

- What can you do when something unfair happens to you?

- How can you help someone else who has something unfair happen?

Consider reading *The Cow That Went Oink* by Bernard Most when you play this game. Find out more on page 63.

Focus on Assets
27: Equality and Social Justice
28: Integrity

Backward Dress

Time: 5 minutes

Have the children take off their shoes. On a count of three, have them all put their shoes on the wrong feet, stand up, and carefully walk backward to sit in their seat. Because it's backward, the last one to complete the task gets a point.

Let's Talk

- How did it feel to walk in the wrong shoes?

- Have you ever told a lie or said the wrong thing? How did you feel when you did that?

- In this game, all you had to do to make something right was put your shoes on the right feet. What do you do in real life to make wrong things right?

- In this game the team who finished last was the winner. Was that fair?

Focus on Assets
27: Equality and Social Justice
29: Honesty

Backward Lineup

Time: 5 minutes

Have everyone state his birthday date (without the month). Challenge the children to line up backward from the 31st to the 1st within two minutes.

Variation: Using different information, have the children line up backward by birthday month (December to January), last letter of their first name (Z–A), height (tallest to shortest), and so on.

Let's Talk

- Has anyone ever thought something about you that wasn't true? Did they tell other people (spread gossip)? How did you feel about that?

- What can you do if someone thinks something about you that isn't true?

- How can you make sure you don't think the wrong things about other people?

- What should you do if you hear something about a friend, and you know it isn't true?

- In this game the team who finished last was the winner. Was that fair?

Focus on Assets
29: Honesty
30: Responsibility
33: Interpersonal Competence
37: Personal Power

Over/Under Pass

Time: 5–10 minutes

You Will Need: One paper wad or soft, spongy ball per team

Divide the group and have them stand in two to three lines. Have everyone face forward. Give the person at the *back* of each line a paper wad or ball. Have those players pass the ball over the head to the person directly in front of them. Children should continue to pass the ball up the entire line. Once the ball reaches the end, play pauses to prepare for the next pass. This time, have everyone stand in a riding-horse stance (legs spread apart). Have the first person in each line start and hand the ball under her legs to the person behind her. Children should continue passing the ball until it reaches the end of the line. The team that comes in last gets a point.

If your group wants an extra challenge, have everyone stand with her legs spread apart. Start as usual, but alternate over-the-head passes and under-the-leg passes back and forth, all the way to the front of the line and then to the back of the line.

Let's Talk

• In this game, some things came your way that you didn't see coming. Has this ever happened to you in school or at home?

• What can you do if something bad happens all of a sudden?

• What can you do to surprise other people in a good way?

• In this game the team who finished last was the winner. Was that fair?

Focus on Assets
26: Caring
30: Responsibility
32: Planning and Decision Making

OLYMPICS

Note: All of the Olympic games can be played as individual events or with representatives from each team.

Disc Throw

Time: 10 minutes

You Will Need: Paper plates, crayons

Each team or individual should decorate their "disc" (a paper plate) so that they can easily identify it after each throw in the trial. Have players line up behind a starting line. (If playing in teams, have each team send one representative to the starting line.) At your direction, have the Olympians throw their paper plate as far as they can. Have volunteers stand where each one falls. Allow players two chances for a personal best. Best distance overall wins.

Javelin Throw

Time: 5 minutes

You Will Need: Straws or Q-tips

This is another event in which farthest distance wins. Have players line up behind a starting line and throw their javelin straws as far as they can. Have volunteers stand where each javelin falls. Players get two chances for a personal best. Best distance overall wins.

Frisbee Throw

Time: 5 minutes (actual game time, does not include Frisbee preparation)

You Will Need: Popsicle sticks, glue, a trash can

Preparation: Have children make Frisbees a day or two before the actual event. Each child should use 6 to 12 Popsicle sticks and weave them together, keeping them evenly spaced, then use glue to keep them together. Allow a day or two to dry thoroughly. In the first round, players should throw their Frisbee for distance in order for you to declare a winner. For a second round, have players toss their Frisbee for accuracy. Have them aim toward shooting their Frisbee into a trash can. Any Frisbees that fall apart are disqualified.

Long Jump

Time: 5 minutes

Have each individual Olympian jump straight ahead, keeping both feet together. Have someone stand at the spot where the person jumped to mark his distance. Each player gets two opportunities to jump for an individual best. Best distance among the entire group wins the event.

Variation: Use a measuring tape to measure and record each individual jump and determine personal bests, as well as the overall event winner.

Long Jump Relay

Time: 5–10 minutes

This activity is a little twist on the long jump, with the best distance determined by teams. Divide the group into smaller teams. Remind participants that this is the long jump, so when they jump they must keep their feet together. The first person from each team lines up behind the starting line and on "go," they all jump as far as they can. The next person from each team stands where her team leader landed and takes her jump from there. The third player takes his place where the second player landed and jumps from there. Continue in this manner until all players have jumped. The team that has collectively jumped the farthest wins.

Jumping Frog Variation

Time: 5 minutes

Divide the group into teams. Have each team start from a squatting-down position with hands on the ground (like a frog). Each person will jump up and forward from the frog position and land with feet together and hands forward and touching the ground. As in the previous game, the next person in line will replace the first and continue on until all players have jumped. The team that has the best collective distance wins.

Let's Talk

- Which activities did you like best—the ones where you did things all by yourself or the ones where you worked with a team? Why?

- What are some things you are able to do all by yourself?

- How does it feel to be able to do things all by yourself?

- What are some things you do better when you work with others?

• Why is it important to learn to work together?

Consider reading *Koala Lou* by Mem Fox when you do any of these Olympic activities. See page 93.

Focus on Assets
31: Self-Regulation
37: Personal Power
38: Self-Esteem

MARATHON EVENTS

These events offer a variety of endurance and "going the distance" activities. They can be performed by individuals or as teams, with members choosing a representative for each event.

Time: 15–30 minutes

You Will Need: A watch or timer

Jumping Jacks
The winner is the player who can do the most jumping jacks in a set amount of time.

Running in Place
The winner is the player who can sustain running in place for the longest time.

Sit-Ups
The winner is the player who can do the most sit-ups in a set amount of time.

Push-Ups
The winner is the player who can do the most push-ups in a set amount of time.

Squats
The winner is the player who can do the most squats in a given time.

Nonstop Talking
The winner is the player who can talk non-stop for the longest period of time, without a significant break in chatting.

Joke Telling
The winner is the player who can tell the most jokes in one minute.

Stare-Downs
The elimination rounds start in pairs. The first person to look away (and/or laugh, if you want to add this rule) is out. One winner from each pair goes on to form new pairs until an overall stare-down winner is determined.

Variation: Have a staring-without-blinking contest to see who can hold her eyes open the longest.

Let's Talk

• This game lets people show that they have different gifts, like talking, staring, telling jokes, and running. What are other things you are good at doing?

• Do you have a special gift or talent? What is it?

• Is there a skill or talent that you'd like to learn more about?

• If you played as a team, how did you decide which person would do each event?

Focus on Assets
31: Self-Regulation
37: Personal Power
38: Self-Esteem

Bet You Can't Be Quiet!

Time: 5 minutes

You Will Need: A watch or timer

Introduce the challenge: who can be quiet for 30 seconds? Bring three to five contestants up front. Ask the rest of the group if they think these players can do it or not. Ask for a volunteer to be the challenger. Say: *Who wants to try to make these contestants break their silence by making them talk, laugh, giggle, or snort within 30 seconds?* Once you have a challenger, start the clock and time the players. See how long they can go without reacting audibly to their challenger. Repeat as often as you like. Extend the 30-second time limit for extremely good players.

Let's Talk

• Why are both laughter and quiet times important in our lives?

• What are some examples of times when laughter was especially good and fun, or when laughter helped make a situation better?

• Are there times when laughter has made a situation worse?

• What are some examples of times when being quiet or having quiet feels good or is important?

Consider pairing this activity with the book *A Quiet Place* by Douglas Wood. See more about this story on page 76.

Focus on Assets
37: Personal Power
38: Self-Esteem

SCAVENGER HUNTS

Holiday Scavenger Hunt

Time: 15 minutes

Celebrate holidays by hunting for colors. On Valentine's Day, hunt for red items. On St. Patrick's Day, hunt for green items. On the Fourth of July, hunt for red, white, and blue objects. Hunts can be done individually, in pairs, or in teams. Give children 5–10 minutes to go and find as many items as possible that have the specified color. Limit them to bringing back one of each type of item. (For example, one blade of grass unless they can find two distinct colors, such as green grass and brown grass.) Award points for the number of items found (1 each), and extra points, 5 each, for the most unique color and the most unique item.

Note: For safety purposes, limit where children can go on their hunt to a space supervised by adult or teen observers. If time is a concern, you can also limit where they go to the room you are in, a specific hallway, outdoor play area, and so on.

Let's Talk

• What was your favorite item that you found? Why?

• What colors make you feel happy? Sad?

- What would life be like if we had only one color for everything?

- People are like colors, varied and different. How can we appreciate the good things in every person?

Focus on Assets
32: Planning and Decision Making
33: Interpersonal Competence

News Scavenger Hunt

Time: 5–10 minutes

You Will Need: A pre-generated list of objects to find, crayons, newspapers and/or magazines

Separate the group into teams and give each a list of objects to look for in the newspapers or magazines you've provided. Have them highlight their finds by circling them with a crayon. Tell them they can circle either pictures or words that represent the items on the list. (For younger children who cannot yet read, you may want them to circle only pictures.) The team with the most items found in a designated time period wins.

Variation 1: Call out items one at a time. The team that finds that item in the newspaper or magazine first brings it up to you to show you. If their find is correct, they win that round. Continue for a set number of rounds, usually 5 to 10.

Variation 2: Follow the same instructions in the regular activity or Variation 1, but use comic strips instead of newspapers or magazines.

Let's Talk

- Have you ever looked at newspapers or magazines before?

- What do you usually notice when you look at them?

- How did this activity help you look at newspapers or magazines in a different way?

- Did you like using crayons and highlighters for this activity? How can artwork help your schoolwork?

Focus on Assets
17: Creative Activities
25: Reading for Pleasure

These-Two-Things Scavenger Hunt

Time: 15–20 minutes

You Will Need: A pre-generated list of items—one copy of the list per team

Create a list of items for players to find either outside or inside. (Include compare-and-contrast items and the point values they are worth. See the examples below.) Have the children form teams and instruct them to find the items listed. Set a time limit for their treasure hunt (5–10 minutes). Let children know how points will be awarded. The number of points each item receives is based on two criteria: (1) having the item—5 points, and (2) how the items compare and contrast with each other (see examples below). (You can determine the points for compare and contrast.) You may want to take a group vote to determine the point winner for some objects, such as most colorful leaf or smelliest flower.

For example, your list might include:

- The strongest flower and the most fragile flower (10 points each)

- The longest grass blade and the shortest grass blade (5 points each)

- The largest rock and the smallest rock (10 points each)

- A stick with the pointiest end (15 points)

- The most colorful leaf (5 points)

- The smelliest flower (10 points)

No matter the object, you can emphasize the compare-and-contrast aspect, for example, comparing large rock to large rock, and contrasting largest rock to smallest rock. This allows players to really look for and take in details on the objects they've collected. Playing outdoors connects them more deeply with nature and helps them appreciate its treasures.

Note: For safety purposes, make sure you have enough adult or older-teen observers to supervise players if they conduct their search outside.

Let's Talk

- How much did you want to win this activity?

- Which is more important, winning or doing your best even if you don't win?

- In what ways do you compare yourself to other people? Is that a good thing to do? Why?

- What makes you special?

Focus on Assets
21: Achievement Motivation

ASSET INDEX

Achievement Motivation, 37, 72, 74, 116, 119, 120, 122, 123, 128, 134, 147

Adult Role Models, 30, 68, 99, 104, 132

Bonding to School, 40, 116

Caring, 31, 63, 64, 86, 88, 91, 92, 98, 100, 103, 108, 113, 114, 115, 117, 118, 125, 129, 132, 133, 137, 142

Caring Neighborhood, 27, 66, 86, 94, 98, 105, 134

Caring School Climate, 35, 114, 115, 117, 118, 119, 120, 127, 134

Child Programs, 44

Children as Resources, 22, 96, 127, 129

Community Values Children, 28, 89

Creative Activities, 43, 64, 65, 71, 74, 78, 81, 82, 87, 88, 89, 103, 123, 124, 129, 130, 131, 146

Cultural Competence, 56, 60, 61, 69, 73, 75, 78, 93, 95, 96, 103, 109, 110, 115, 117, 123, 131, 134

Equality and Social Justice, 32, 63, 94, 141

Family Boundaries, 23, 61, 68, 69, 71, 72, 100, 101, 127

Family Support, 19, 60, 61, 64, 67, 71, 77, 88, 93, 94, 96, 97, 98, 99, 101, 102, 104–07, 109

Healthy Lifestyle, 118

High Expectations, 42, 74, 86, 96, 98, 100, 120, 122, 123, 126, 128

Honesty, 48, 67, 108, 113, 121, 131, 141, 142

Integrity, 47, 68, 75, 92, 95, 113, 117, 121, 124, 126, 127, 138, 141

Interpersonal Competence, 34, 62, 63, 64, 66, 71, 75, 78, 86, 89, 91, 92, 95, 98, 99, 100, 101, 103, 105, 108, 113, 114, 115, 117, 118, 121, 122, 123, 125, 129, 136, 139, 142, 146

Neighborhood Boundaries, 29, 69, 98

Other Adult Relationships, 26, 64, 65, 68, 84, 86, 98, 104, 106

Parent Involvement in Schooling, 21

Peaceful Conflict Resolution, 51, 62, 91, 92, 95, 99, 100, 138

Personal Power, 52, 63, 65, 72, 77, 79, 83, 88, 90, 91, 96, 102, 103, 104, 106, 109, 110, 120, 121, 124, 125, 128, 131, 132, 133, 134, 137, 138, 140, 142, 144, 145

Planning and Decision Making, 49, 61, 63, 70, 72, 74, 75, 88, 93, 106, 116, 117, 119, 120, 121, 122, 125, 128, 132, 140, 142, 146

Positive Family Communication, 20, 93, 96, 97, 99, 101, 102, 106, 109

Positive Peer Influence, 41, 66, 97, 115, 117, 127, 132, 136, 139

Positive View of Personal Future, 58, 76, 77, 79, 84, 88, 91, 94, 99, 102, 103, 104, 110, 124, 132, 138

Reading for Pleasure, 46, 87, 105, 146
Religious Community, 45
Resistance Skills, 50, 127, 138
Responsibility, 25, 67, 73, 75, 97, 100, 101, 127, 136, 137, 138, 140, 142

Safety, 55, 69, 104, 126, 140
School Boundaries, 36, 72, 73, 101, 126, 127
School Engagement, 38, 81, 118, 120, 123, 128
Self-Esteem, 57, 60, 62, 63, 64, 65, 66, 71, 72, 76, 79, 80, 83, 91, 93, 95, 109, 110, 113, 114, 115, 131, 138, 139, 140, 144, 145
Self-Regulation, 33, 50, 73, 83, 85, 93, 127, 133, 139, 140, 144, 145
Sense of Purpose, 53, 74, 76, 79, 84, 90, 102, 109, 113, 114, 127, 132, 133, 138, 139
Service to Others, 54, 75, 129, 137

Time at Home, 24, 76, 87

ABOUT THE AUTHORS

Susan Ragsdale and **Ann Saylor** are nationally recognized trainers, speakers, authors, and consultants in the youth and community development field. As co-founders of the Center for Asset Development at the YMCA of Middle Tennessee, they have coached and trained numerous youth-serving agencies and schools on developing and empowering youth leaders, team building, service-learning, program strategies, and youth development best practices. They have published two books together—*Great Group Games: 175 Boredom-Busting, Zero-Prep Team Builders for All Ages* and *Ready to Go Service Projects: 140 Ways for Youth Groups to Lend a Hand.* They have a passion for empowering youth to succeed and sustaining professionals in the youth development field, and they share common interests in reading for fun, bringing play into their work and homes, and creative self-expression—however that may play out.

Susan Ragsdale has been doing youth and community development work with the YMCA of Middle Tennessee since 1992. Her work includes a variety of teen leadership and inner-city outreach programs, both locally and nationally with the YMCA of USA, ranging from directing a regional youth environmental service-learning program to helping coach the "Bulldawgs" inner-city team. Susan lives in Nashville with her husband, Pete, and their two dogs.

Ann Saylor has developed and directed youth programs for multiple organizations—including Points of Light Foundation, Tennessee 4-H, Volunteer Tennessee, and Harpeth Hall School since 1994. She has published more than 150 articles about youth leadership, service-learning, Developmental Assets, and personal balance as well as putting her theories to work both in the classroom and in the community. Ann and her husband Dan have three children, Daniel, Brendan, and Anna Kate, and live in Pleasant View, Tennessee.

If you would like to know more about the authors or their work in youth and community development, go to theassetedge.net. They offer in-services, workshops, and retreats for educators, youth workers, and children in various positive-youth-development practices.

Susan and Ann would like to invite you to share with others your favorite books, games, and activities for promoting creativity and sparking the imagination by visiting their blog, which can be found at

theassetedge.blogspot.com